THE INNER RUNNING AND THE OUTER RUNNING

YOGIC SECRETS FOR BETTER RUNNING

SRI CHINMOY

AUM PUBLICATIONS NEW YORK

This volume is a compilation of Sri Chinmoy's talks, conversations, poems and answers to questions on running, representing a thirty-year span from the inception of the Sri Chinmoy Marathon Team in 1977 until his passing in 2007.

Sri Chinmoy's first book, ***Meditations: Food for the Soul,*** was published in 1970.

Copyright © 2008 Sri Chinmoy Centre

ISBN 978-1-934972-02-1

All rights reserved. No portion of this book may be reproduced without express written permission of the Publisher. Printed in the U.S.A.

Aum Publications
86-10 Parsons Blvd.
Jamaica, New York 11432
www.srichinmoybooks.com

Dedication to Jesse Owens

Spirituality means speed: speed in the inner world, speed in the outer world. In the inner world, speed is founded mostly upon aspiration. In the outer world, speed is founded mostly upon inspiration.

There are some individuals who have speed in the inner world, while there are others who have speed in the outer world. There are few, very few, who have speed both in the inner world and in the outer world. Jesse Owens, the champion of champions, the immortal of immortals, had this rare speed both in the inner world and in the outer world. He is the colossal pride of the entire America.

Finally, he is, indeed, a universal treasure. As the outer world treasures his fastest speed, even so, the inner world cherishes his bravest dedication that fought against poverty, darkness and ignorance in human life. He has contributed abundant speed and light to the entire world.

—*Sri Chinmoy*

Contents

Foreword by Carl Lewis viii

Introduction by Ted Corbitt x

The Inner Running and the Outer Running 1

Training 17

Racing 27

Fatigue and Injuries 47

Masters-Category Runners 57

Advice to Carl Lewis 65

Advice to Paul Tergat 81

Questions from Champion Runners 85

Interviews with Journalists 105

The Inner Runner 127

Running and the Life Game 137

My Daily Running Experiences 145

Appendix: Biographical Notes on Champion Runners 161

Foreword

Having retired from competition in 1997, I am no longer running and jumping my way around the world. But after representing America on five Olympic track-and-field teams—from 1980 to 1996—I certainly can feel and know what today's Olympic hopefuls are doing and thinking.

For them I would like to offer this book, *The Inner Running and the Outer Running: Yogic Secrets for Better Running.*

For me the Olympics are embodied in one of my favorite notions from Sri Chinmoy: "All athletes should bear in mind that they are competing not with other athletes but with their own capacities." I turned to this notion whenever I needed an injection of the competitive fire.

Many people may not be aware of it, but I have known Sri Chinmoy, the Indian spiritual teacher, for my whole Olympic career. His spiritual Centre in New York is almost like home to me. Every time I was in the area, I visited Sri Chinmoy. He and many of his students came to the 1984, 1988, 1992 and 1996 Olympics to support me.

My relationship with Sri Chinmoy started spiritually, because he was so loving, positive and uplifting. That inspiration helped me with my track and field club, with my teammates and in my relationships. In later years he inspired me to continue on with my athletic career. Sri Chinmoy was a sprinter in his youth; in his forties he was a marathon runner and when he was 55 years old he became a weightlifter. When I saw Sri Chinmoy at his age lifting weights and lifting cars, I felt I had to evolve as a person and as an athlete.

When I became 30 or 35 years old, I always heard how old I was. Even though every single day I would hear, "You are too old, you can't do it," I really stayed focused on what I could do.

FOREWORD

And when I won a second gold medal in the 100 metres in 1988, I was the oldest gold medallist and the only one to repeat that win. When I set the world record in the 100 metres in 1991, I was the oldest world-record holder for that event. In the long jump in Atlanta I was the oldest long jump champion. Sri Chinmoy has shown me that if you just follow the Supreme in yourself and also challenge yourself, there really are no limits.

Believe me, the joy that comes from "going beyond" is the most incredible feeling in the world. I have felt it many times. And I have enjoyed watching others experience it.

The ultimate joy comes from performing one's absolute best, no matter one's order of finish.

—*Carl Lewis*

Carl Lewis and Sri Chinmoy at their first meeting in New York (1983).

Introduction

This book is meant to serve as an inspiration for runners, other athletes and those interested in sports and physical fitness. It aims to encourage people to become more keenly interested in their own overall development: physically, psychically and spiritually.

Here we see the evolving teachings of spiritual guide Sri Chinmoy—the philosophy that he and his students practise, along with their meditation activities, to achieve self-fulfilment and more dynamic lives. Rather than offer a "how to" manual, Sri Chinmoy is sharing his and his students' experiences in integrating meditation and sports activities (particularly long-distance running) to enhance the quality of their lives. For them, running and the spiritual world are closely related.

Sri Chinmoy was born and raised in India, where he originally nurtured his interests in meditation and spiritual activities, and where he first competed in athletics (decathlon and sprints). He then became the spiritual teacher of meditation students in many countries of the world, until his passing in 2007.

Sri Chinmoy stressed running as an allegory for the spiritual life. But then he also told his students to really go out and run. In his own revived athletic career, Sri Chinmoy ran a lot himself, averaging up to 100 miles a week at times. A knee injury limited his running in his later years, but he still kept his love for running and encouraged his students to continue with the sport. For he believed that running and other physical activities can be used as an aid in the spiritual awakening of spiritual seekers. This book reflects his answers to runners' questions over several decades.

Sri Chinmoy's yoga is that of self-transcendence. Sri Chinmoy has said, "When we transcend any aspect of ourselves, our spiritual qualities grow and expand. ... We are all truly unlimited, if we only dare to try and have faith." This explains, in part, the motto of the Sri Chinmoy Marathon Team: "Run and become. Become and run."

Sri Chinmoy Marathon Team runners have sponsored many races for the public, ranging from two miles to marathons and triathlons, and, more recently, ultramarathons up to 3100 miles. Also, they have gone out of their way to help local running communities stage their own races. The Sri Chinmoy runners are not seeking to become champion runners as much as to garner the best within themselves.

A wonder of this period in history is the relatively enormous and growing interest in long-distance running, and the involvement in running of so many diverse peoples around the world. While not everyone can become a champion runner, almost every runner can manage to make some progress if he or she seeks it.

Those who meditate feel the same way about their search for self-perfection. Indeed, today there is also an exceptional interest in meditation for its own sake. Sri Chinmoy's students, seeking inner peace, feel that regular meditation helps to clear the mind of doubt and anxiety, enhances spiritual progress and encourages the body to wake up and live.

The Sri Chinmoy Marathon Team and its spiritual leader Sri Chinmoy—a unique group of people—have explored many facets of meditation and running. This book gives all an opportunity to study their experiences.

—*Ted Corbitt*

Ted Corbitt was considered "The Father of Long Distance Running" (see biographical information in the Appendix). He completed this introduction before his earthly journey ended on 13 December 2007, just two months after Sri Chinmoy's passing.

1
THE INNER RUNNING
AND THE OUTER RUNNING

Each human being is travelling along Eternity's Road.

Prayer and meditation always remind us of our inner running. The only difference between the outer running and the inner running is that in the inner running there is no set goal or destination. In the outer running, as soon as we have finished one hundred metres, let us say, the race is over. We may not win, but we have reached our goal. But in the inner running, we are Eternity's runners.

Our inner running definitely helps us in our outer running. Through prayer and meditation, we can develop intense will-power, and this will-power can help us do extremely well in our outer running. Meditation is stillness, calmness, quietness, while the running consciousness is all dynamism. Again, the runner's outer speed has a special kind of poise or stillness at its very heart. In fact, the outer life, the outer movement, can be successful only when it comes from the inner poise. If there is no poise, then there can be no successful outer movement. Poise is an unseen power, and this unseen power is always ready to come to the aid of the outer runner.

The inner runner is always trying to inspire the outer runner. First the inner runner says, "Go forward, go forward! Go ahead, go ahead!" The outer runner says, "How can I go ahead if you do not give me the aspiration and inner cry?" Then the inner runner gives the outer runner the inner cry to do something great and to become something good. In this way, the inner runner offers inspiration and aspiration to the outer runner.

> The outer run
> And the inner run
> Are two complementary souls.
> They help each other
> Tremendously.

Are people turning to running nowadays as a kind of supplement to their spiritual lives?

Many people have discovered that running is a most effective way to bring about happiness. Running demands not only the fitness of the body but the fitness of the vital,* mind and heart as well. Sometimes the body is fit enough to run, but the mind is not ready. Again, sometimes the mind wants to run, but the body does not want to co-operate. When it is a matter of running, all the "members of the family"—the body, vital, mind and heart— have to work together. Through running, the soul wants to offer a feast to all its children. Its joy will not be complete if even one member—the body, vital, mind or heart—does not participate. What running is doing is keeping the body, vital, mind and heart fit so that the soul can get complete happiness.

How can we benefit spiritually from training for and running marathons?

Long-distance running gives us a real feeling of accomplishment. Speed and endurance are both important, specially in the spiritual life. If one has only speed, then one cannot ultimately succeed; we need endurance because the goal is quite far. Again, if one has only stamina and no speed, then it will take forever to reach the goal. Only if someone has both qualities will he be able to make very good progress in his spiritual life and achieve something really great in life.

Just as the marathon is a long journey on the outer plane, so is spirituality a long, longer, longest journey in the inner plane. When you run a marathon, you are trying to accomplish on the physical plane something most difficult and arduous. When you

---

*'Vital' is a term used in Indian philosophy for the aspect of human nature that embodies emotional and aggressive or dynamic qualities.

do this, it gives you joy because it reminds you of what you are trying to accomplish in the inner plane. As you are determined to complete the longest journey on the outer plane, the marathon, so are you determined to reach the Goal in your inner journey. The outer journey will always remind you of your inner journey towards God-realisation, and the inner journey will remind you of your outer journey towards God-manifestation.

What is your philosophy about the outer life and the inner life?

We try to synthesise and harmonise the outer life and the inner life. The outer life is like a beautiful flower and the inner life is its fragrance. If there is no fragrance, then we cannot appreciate the flower. Again, if there is no flower, how can there be any fragrance? So the inner life and the outer life must go together.

> My outer running shows me
> The smiling Face of God.
> My inner running brings me
> The dancing Heart of God.

Why do you, as a spiritual Teacher, run?

My running shows my students that I am not a so-called Indian philosopher who lives in the moon land and has nothing to do with reality. It reminds them that I not only preach and teach but also act.

I know that my running has increased and will continue to increase the eagerness of my good students to make both inner and outer progress. I not only encourage my students to do things that will benefit them inwardly and outwardly, but I also do these things myself in order to offer them inspiration.

Also, right from my childhood, I have had tremendous determination. When I reach a certain standard, if it is the Will of the

Supreme that I reach only that particular height, then I give up. Otherwise, I never give up. I continue, continue, continue, all the time trying to transcend my previous limit. My goal is always to go beyond, beyond, beyond. There are no limits to our capacity, because we have the infinite Divine within us, and the Supreme is always transcending His own Reality-Existence. So my only goal is progress, and there is no end to our progress.

Is there any spiritual benefit from participating in races as opposed to daily training runs?

If you participate in races, it will add to your strength and determination in the inner world. While practising every day, you usually do not have the same kind of determination that you have when you are running a race. While you are in a race, even if you are a poor runner, you are determined to do your best, so you collect some inner strength and determination. This determination immediately enters into the Universal Consciousness and, like wildfire, it spreads. Then, somebody running in Africa or Australia or in some other part of the world will all of a sudden feel a burst of energy, which is coming from you and nobody else.

Which is more important, the running experience or actually winning the race?

Always there should be a goal. Having a goal does not mean that we have to try to defeat the world's top runners. Far from it! Our goal should be our own progress, and progress itself is the most illumining experience.

>   **Always I transcend and transcend.**
>   **How?**
>   **Just by competing only with myself.**

For a serious runner, is there any difference between aspiration and ambition?

There is a great difference between aspiration and ambition. If a runner wants to exert himself to his utmost capacity and reach his best running speed, then that is his aspiration. But when there is ambition, immediately a kind of rivalry starts. Ambition wants to be the best in everything, but aspiration is different. It says, "I will do my best. If I want to engage in sports, I shall have to practise seriously. But I will place the result, the achievement, entirely at the Feet of the Supreme."

How can running energise us inwardly?

While you are running—specially when you are tired—you are much more conscious of your breathing. You are more aware of when you are inhaling and when you are exhaling. While running, when you inhale, you can consciously invoke divine energy to energise you. This divine energy energises the willing reality in you and illumines the unlit reality in you. When you breathe in the divine energy, automatically it transforms undivine forces into divine forces.

Each time you breathe in, if you can repeat just one time God's Name or 'Supreme' or whatever divine name or form comes to mind, then that spiritual thought will increase your purity. Then, when you breathe out, feel that a new promise is going out from you to the Universal Consciousness. This new promise is nothing short of your sincere willingness and eagerness to become a good and perfect instrument of the Supreme.

Can running help get rid of frustration and anger?

Running is an excellent way to rid oneself of frustration and anger. If you are really angry with someone, go and run. After a mile or so you will see that your anger has gone away, either because you are totally exhausted or because the satisfaction that you gain from physical exertion has replaced your anger.

In India, one of my mentors used to say, "If anyone is angry, that person should jog in place." Instead of telling his students to pray to God to take away their anger, he told them to jog. He always said that they did not have to cover any distance—just jog in place. Within a minute or two, all their anger would go away. He knew that running can be an effective method of ridding people of negative emotions.

What is the best mantra for running?

While running, if you can repeat the Name of the Supreme most soulfully and devotedly, then naturally it will help you improve your speed and endurance. If you want a mantra, then 'Supreme' is the best mantra. If you want a special type of meditation, then 'Supreme' is the best type of meditation. Just try to repeat the Name of the Supreme most soulfully. It will help you improve your speed and increase your power of endurance.

When you start running, inwardly write down on the top of your head, "No mind, no mind!" Inside the mind is determination, but inside the heart is will-power, psychic will-power. If you can use the will-power that the mind has in the form of determination, good. But it is no match for the heart's psychic will-power. Do not think of failure; be cheerful. If you failed previously, feel that that day did not exist. Make your mind fresh and clean. Live with new hope and new promise.

> **If we believe in our own**
> **Self-transcendence-task,**
> **Then there can be**
> **No unreachable goal.**

What is the relationship between running and meditation?

Running in the outer life makes us active and dynamic. Also, the outer running reminds us that we must run inwardly. If we can run in the inner world instead of just walking, then our progress will be much faster, and we will reach our goal sooner. So when we run or do physical exercises in order to become strong, healthy and dynamic, these qualities in our outer life help us considerably in our inner life. Again, our prayer and meditation also help us in our running. Through prayer and meditation we can develop intense will-power. This will-power can help us do extremely well in our outer running.

In sports we need energy, strength and dynamism. When we meditate, we make our mind calm and quiet. If inside us there is peace, then we will derive tremendous strength from our inner life. If I have a peaceful moment, even for one second, that peace will come to me as a solid strength in my sports. That strength is almost indomitable strength, whereas if we are restless, we do not have strength like that.

Look at an elephant. An elephant has tremendous strength. It is not restless like a monkey which is moving here and there. It is exactly the same for us. In our inner life if we have the strength of an elephant, then only in our outer life can we be peaceful. But monkeys and other animals that are very, very restless, what kind of strength do they have? Meditation gives us inner strength. Once we have inner strength, we are bound to be successful in our outer life.

Our philosophy does not negate either the outer life or the inner life. Most human beings negate the inner life. They feel that the inner life is not important as long as they can exist on earth. Again, there are a few who think that the outer life is not necessary. They feel that the best thing is to enter into the Himalayan caves and lead a life of solitude, since the outer life is so painful and full of misunderstanding.

We do not believe in living either a life of solitude or an ordinary human life—the so-called modern life that depends on machines and not on the inner reality, the soul.

> Before you enter into
> The whirlpool of activities,
> Calm your mind.
> Then success and progress
> Will be all yours.

Is running better for a seeker than other forms of exercise?

Running is undoubtedly better for a seeker than other forms of strenuous exercise. First of all, running reminds us of our inner journey to self-knowledge. When we run—specially when we run long distances—we are more aware of this inner goal than we are while doing other forms of strenuous exercise. When we run a marathon, we are trying to accomplish something very difficult and arduous on the physical plane. This long outer journey reminds us of our long inner journey towards self-knowledge. One of the reasons a marathon run gives us such inner joy is because it reminds us of what we are trying to accomplish inwardly. The one journey will always remind us of the other. The outer journey will remind us of our inner journey towards God-realisation, and the inner journey will remind us of our outer journey towards God-manifestation. Running not only reminds us of our goal but it also makes us aware of our determination and our need to reach the goal.

A second reason that running is better for us is because other forms of strenuous exercise sometimes totally destroy our enthusiasm. Running, on the other hand, makes us feel that we are making constant progress. Every inch, every metre that we progress is taking us closer to our goal, so naturally it is easier to maintain our enthusiasm.

Even on the outer plane running is better because, thirdly, it gives us exercise from the soles of our feet to the crown of our head. From top to bottom, we get exercise.

From the inner point of view and from the outer point of view, running is infinitely better for us than even the most difficult forms of strenuous exercise. Other kinds of exercise are good, but if they are too strenuous, they may tell upon our health. If we run, however, we will make both inner and outer progress.

What are the best qualities of running as opposed to playing tennis?

Running reminds us of our inner journey, which is ahead of us. The goal is ahead and we are running towards the goal. It is a great feeling, which eventually grows into a great achievement.

Playing tennis reminds us of being an instrument. The tennis ball is a self-giving instrument, always trying to please us in our own way. Whichever way we want to strike it, the tennis ball listens to us. So tennis reminds us of our divine goal, which is to become a perfect instrument of God and to please God in His own Way, and running reminds us of our continuous journey along Eternity's Road towards the Destined Goal.

Tennis and running are like two paths going to the same Goal; they both ultimately reach the Goal, but they reach it from different directions.

I consider myself a tennis player, not a runner. On the one hand, I get more joy from playing tennis, but on the other hand, I get more satisfaction if I run a marathon. Why is this?

You can play tennis for hours and hours. It is easy for you to do well and you enjoy it. But people get more satisfaction from doing the thing that they find most difficult. On the one hand, we like to do things that are easy. On the other hand, we also want the joy that comes from doing whatever is most difficult.

THE INNER RUNNING AND THE OUTER RUNNING

The grass is always greener on the other side. To accomplish something that is more difficult for us to do gives us much more joy. If we have a tennis ball to play with, we will start looking for a basketball, just because we do not have one. But if we had a basketball, we would start looking for a tennis ball. Again, some people will say that they need both a tennis ball and a basketball.

There is also another aspect to this. Even though we may want to run only 100 metres, we want to get the glory that comes from running a marathon. When somebody runs a marathon, he is appreciated and admired. So we feel that a marathon is more important than a 100-metre run. The most difficult thing impresses us most. This is human nature.

Does it give the same benefit to the body and spiritual life to play tennis as it does to run?

I will never say that running is better than tennis. If you accept the inner philosophy of tennis, which is "love and serve", then you can derive so much benefit. Also, tennis can give us so much joy because we are playing with someone and there are so many different movements of the body. Tennis is an excellent form of recreation. When you are playing tennis, you are getting so much innocent joy. Because of your joy, you are becoming like a child once more, and that happiness itself is helping you to make progress.

But I wish to say that running has its own inner value, which tennis cannot offer you. While you run, each breath that you take is connected with a higher reality. While you are jogging, if you are in a good consciousness, your breath is being blessed by a higher inner breath. Of course, while you are jogging if you are chatting with one of your friends about mundane things, then this will not apply. But if you are in a good consciousness while you are running, each breath will connect you with a higher, deeper, inner reality.

Running also has a special symbolic meaning. In the spiritual life, we are eternal runners, running along Eternity's Road. We do not say that we are eternal tennis players on that road. These are two different subjects, like history and geography. If you can do both, if you can run two or three miles a day and play tennis as well, then you will get benefit from being both the eternal runner and the eternal server. But if you have to make a choice, and if you like tennis more than you like running, then you have only to play tennis. Again, if you want to get the benefit of a higher force or higher reality for your physical body, then running is absolutely necessary. I am not saying that you have to run the fastest. Even while jogging, you can feel that you have two breaths. One is a higher breath. Something is pulling you up or you are carrying yourself up. The other is your body's breath. The two are combined together.

> My outer running
> Is my body's journey—
> The destination is known.
> My inner running
> Is my soul's journey—
> The Goal is unknowable.

I have a hard time finding joy in running. Do you think if I play tennis it will help my running?

Tennis will never help your running, far from it. But running will help your tennis, specially if it is sprinting. Stretching exercises and speed work definitely will help your tennis. That is what Arthur Ashe did. Again, if you want to play five sets, if you want to become a world champion tennis player, then you need stamina. For that you have to practise long distance running.

Tennis is not going to help your running speed, that is absurd. But if running does not give you joy and tennis gives you joy, then you can play tennis for joy.

What does your slogan mean: "Run and Become, Become and Run"?

If we run, we see our capacities becoming fully manifested. Previously our capacities were dormant; they did not function inside us. But when we run, we bring to the fore our hidden capacities and are able to do something and become something.

But once we have become something, that is not the end. Still we have to go forward, because we are eternal pilgrims. Everything in us is transcending. It is like a child. To learn the alphabet is his first goal. He studies and learns it. But will he then give up? No. His second goal is to go to school. Then he wants to go to college.

A runner brings forward his capacity and becomes something. Then he sees some champion runners, and he gets the inspiration to try to become an excellent runner. Perhaps he will one day excel and go beyond them. So there are always higher goals even after we have become something. Once we reach our first goal, we have to run towards a higher goal.

> **Run and become.**
> **Become and run.**
> **Run to succeed in the outer world.**
> **Become to proceed in the inner world.**

Does the concentration that athletes use help them in any way spiritually?

Although their concentration is in the physical plane and the vital plane and not in the psychic plane, still it does help. It is a power, like money-power, which can be applied to any purpose. But if you want to buy something subtle, with money-power you cannot do it. For subtle things you need a different type of concentration.

There is a great difference between psychic concentration and physical or vital concentration. Psychic concentration is really difficult—much more difficult than physical or vital concentration. It is like the elder brother. But the younger brother can definitely help the elder brother. The concentration-power that you learn from athletics will definitely add to your psychic concentration. And if someone has psychic concentration as well as physical concentration, vital concentration and mental concentration, then that person can easily be a great champion in the athletic world as well as in the spiritual world.

Is the practice of sports contrary to spiritual tradition?

There are many Indian ashrams where they say that running is not meant for spiritual people. But in the ancient tradition, in the time of the Vedas and the Mahabharata, sages and seekers practised archery and they were physically strong. Then came an era for lethargy-prone people, so spirituality was very nicely separated from the physical, the vital and the mind. Some spiritual Teachers created a big gap between the two and said, "If you are spiritual, you cannot do physical things, and if you are physically active, you cannot pray and meditate." But we say, "No, spirituality can be in the physical and the physical can be in the spiritual." This is our philosophy.

If you pray in the morning and then go out running, then everything you are doing together. This moment you are taking a step with your left leg; the next moment, with your right leg.

Inwardly you are concentrating and outwardly you are taking exercise. So for you, the body and the soul are going together.

Does meditation distract you when you are racing?

When I used in run the 100-metre dash, in a matter of 11.7 seconds, God knows how many times I meditated on Him. I stood first in the running race, yet while standing first my mind was on God. You may say, "How could you be thinking of God so devotedly? If your mind is on God, you will change lanes on the track and be disqualified." But no, I did it.

How can I try my best in a race without being too competitive?

Do not regard your competitors as opponents. Try only to do your best and only think of your speed. During the race, as soon as you think of someone else, you are entering into his consciousness and your own consciousness you are losing. Even when you just look at him, you are entering into his consciousness. But if you only think of your goal, then you are entering into God's Consciousness and God is helping you. If you keep your own determination then God will come and help you. But if you think of your opponent, then your determination will be divided and a part of your will-power will enter into the other runners. You look at them and then you are surprised or shocked. When you are shocked a certain force arises and this force then enters into the other runners. It is easy for me to talk, but I only wish to express my sympathy and remind you that the next time, even if someone is four metres ahead, this person is not your goal. The finish line remains your goal. It is only there where you will be able to feel God's Grace.

Do not enter
Into the world
Of comparison.
Just dare to better
Yourself every day
Without fail.

2
TRAINING

Coaches should bring to the fore their own inspiration, aspiration, dedication, determination and will-power and offer these capacities to their athletes.

How can I go faster?

To a great extent, speed in running starts in the mind. Try to develop more imagination. Imagine that you are running fast, and appreciate your speed. Then let the thrill and joy that you get from your imagination inundate you. This joy in itself will increase your speed. You can also think of some people who really do run fast and try to identify yourself with them.

> **Life is velocity.**
> **Therefore, I want to run fast, very fast.**

How do you keep your enthusiasm when you start to get tired and exhausted during running?

In short distances—from 100 metres to a mile—it is easy to maintain enthusiasm. You get a burst of energy or inspiration and you go. But for long distances, to maintain enthusiasm is very difficult. There are many, many ways to keep your enthusiasm when you are getting tired in long distance, but here are two ways that are particularly effective.

While running, do not think of yourself as twenty-five or thirty years old. Only think of yourself as six or seven years old. At the age of six or seven, a child does not sit; he just runs here and there. So imagine the enthusiasm of a young child and identify yourself, not with the child, but with the source of his enthusiasm. This is one way.

Another secret way, if you are running long distance, is to identify yourself with ten or even twenty runners who are ahead of you. Only imagine the way they are breathing in and breathing out. Then, while you are inhaling, feel that you are breathing in their own breath and that the energy of the twenty runners is entering into you. Then, while you are exhaling, feel that all twenty runners are breathing out your tiredness and lack of enthusiasm.

While you are running, it may be difficult for you to feel that cosmic energy is entering into you. So occultly or secretly you can try breathing in the breath of twenty runners at a time. The energy which you will receive, which is nothing but enthusiasm, will let you go ten steps forward. But you have to remember that you are breathing in their breath, their inspiration and determination, and not their tiredness. You have to feel that their breath is like pure, distilled water. If you think of someone who is not running well, that person's breath will not help you. But if you think of someone who is running faster than you, his energy will help you. You are not stealing it; only you are taking in the spiritual energy that is all around him and inside him, just as it is inside you. But because he is running faster, you are more conscious of it in him.

Sometimes for days on end I don't feel like running, even though I know it is good for me. How can I overcome this reluctance?

We have to practise self-discipline. It is by doing something, by becoming someone—not necessarily someone great or famous—that we can overcome our reluctance. It is through moving and achieving that we can overcome reluctance. In order to overcome reluctance, we have to try to reach our goal. By always moving and progressing towards a goal, you not only become a better runner but you also become a better instrument of God.

Some days I run much better and faster than others. How can I remain cheerful about my running on days when I cannot run my fastest?

Your running capacity changes every day because every day you are in a different consciousness. One day you feel light. One day you feel heavy. One day you feel inspiration and another day you feel no inspiration. But once you have been running for a while, you develop a basic running capacity, and this capacity will determine how fast you can run even on your slow days. If you normally run a seven-minute mile, then one day if you are not in a dynamic mood, you may go at a nine or ten-minute pace. You will not go at a fourteen or fifteen-minute pace.

On a slow day, if you want to maintain the same joy that you have when you are running well, you can play a trick on yourself. Imagine that instead of being forced to run at a ten-minute pace that day, you decided to run at that pace. If you feel that you have been compelled to run slowly, then you will feel that your freedom has gone away. But if you feel that it was you who commanded your body to go at a ten-minute pace, then you will not feel miserable. Right from the beginning, if you feel that it was your decision to run at that speed, you will be as happy as if you were running at a seven-minute pace.

> I am happy because I have realised
> That the most important thing
> In my life
> Is self-improvement.

How can I get more joy in running?

If you do not get enough joy from running itself, try to bring in some variety. Seven days a week you run, so you can vary your schedule. Do not run each day at the same speed or for the same distance. One day you can run one mile, the second day two miles, the third day seven miles, then again one mile. If you run at seven minutes per mile, then one day go deliberately at a nine-minute pace. The next day do something different: 100 metres walk, 100 metres run, 100 metres walk, 200 metres run. In that way, you will develop a different kind of joy and confidence.

That is what I do. In one mile, if you can have all kinds of variation, then you may get joy. I find that variation gives me tremendous joy. Otherwise, if I have to run one full mile, sometimes it is so boring.

Another day you can run according to your mood. Just let your mind and your heart decide. Perhaps you will run for 20 metres and walk for 200 metres, then again you will run for 800 metres. Allow yourself to be carried by your inspiration. Do not have a fixed distance in mind. Just surrender to your mind's whims. Then afterwards you will get immense joy when you see that you have covered so much distance.

There are so many ways to get joy from running, but if you are badly injured, like me, then there is no way to get joy from running. At that time, just enter into a different field of activity.

Morning running is purity's beauty.
Evening running is simplicity's luminosity.

What time of day is best to run?

It depends on the individual runner. Whenever the individual feels most physically fit, most vitally fit, most mentally fit and most psychically fit is the best time for that individual to run.

I am a morning runner.
God gives me His Beauty.
I am a midday runner.
God gives me His Power.
I am an afternoon runner.
God gives me His Charm.
I am an evening runner.
God gives me His Peace.
I am a midnight runner.
God gives me His Pride.

How careful should I be about choosing a running coach? What qualities should I look for?

Some coaches know many things worth learning, but they lead a very undivine life. Even if someone is a good coach, if he is also full of aggressive, lower vital qualities, then be careful. Indirectly or unconsciously you will invite his undivine qualities into your own life. However, if a coach has some spirituality in him along with his coaching capacity, then consider him.

He does not have to be a student of a spiritual Teacher—far from it. He may be a spiritual person and not even be aware of his spirituality. There are many people like that. If he has goodness, kindness, a clear mind and a sympathetic heart, then he is more than spiritual.

A runner may develop a very strong inner relationship with his coach. Then during the race, if the runner invokes the presence of his coach—his style, his encouragement, his inspiration and dynamic push—at that time the runner can draw extra energy and extra force from his coach.

Again, suppose there is some great runner that you look up to and idolise. Even if this runner is not your coach, if you consciously invoke his or her soul during the race, you can get added strength and added inspiration from that person.

Would you have any message for coaches?

My simple message that I can offer to coaches is to have a oneness-heart with their students. They should try to feel constant oneness not only with their students' outer needs but also with their inner needs. Most coaches help their students outwardly, but they do not help inwardly. If they pray and meditate along with their runners while the runners are competing, they can help their runners considerably. Coaches should practise prayer-life and meditation-life and also encourage their runners to do the same.

On the outer plane many coaches have wisdom; they know much more than their athletes. But if they do not take help from their own inner resources and also help their athletes on the inner plane, then their athletes may not or cannot develop to their greatest potential. Coaches should dive deep within and bring to the fore their own inspiration, aspiration, dedication, determination and will-power and offer these capacities to their athletes. In that way, the athletes and the coaches will work together in their inner lives of aspiration and their outer lives of dedication, and the success they have will be tremendous.

>Who is my coach?
>He who inspires me
>Before I run.
>Who is my coach?
>He who aspires in and through me
>During my run.
>Who is my coach?
>He who corrects and perfects me
>For a better future run.

Sometimes I feel like going out for a run, but something inside holds me back. It's like an inner battle going on. Yet when I do run I feel very happy.

Early in the morning, first the heart says, "Why go out and run? It is time to pray and meditate." Then, after a few minutes, this same heart will have no more energy left to pray and meditate. It will say, "Let me go back to sleep." Then the mind is such a rogue! Whenever the heart is not in tune with the soul, at that time the mind listens to the heart and fully supports the heart. When this kind of separation starts, it is extremely difficult for the body to achieve anything here on earth, on the physical plane.

The body, the vital, the mind, the heart and the soul are

members of the same family and they are supposed to go together. The eldest brother is the soul. Then comes the heart, then the mind, then the vital, then the body. If they stand in line, one after the other, the soul will be able to pull them—like a string. If they are lined up in this way, then it will be very easy for the soul to pull them along.

Unfortunately, it does not happen this way. The soul will go first, but the heart will not be there. Then with greatest difficulty, the soul will run to find where the heart is hiding. Meanwhile, the mind becomes rebellious and revolts. It says, "No, I will not go behind you." Then the vital becomes absolutely stubborn. It says, "No, I am not going at all!"

What will the body do? The poor body wants to go, but it is not getting any inspiration because the vital and mind are not supporting it. The body wants to go with the soul, so that the outer running will go along with the inner running. But the body sees that the mind does not want to go, the vital does not want to go and the heart does not want to go. Then the body starts doubting if it is doing the right thing. The body says, "If I am doing the right thing in following the soul, then how is it that the heart and the mind, my elder brothers, are not doing it? Perhaps I am not doing the right thing. Perhaps the soul is not telling me the right thing."

If the soul says to pray and meditate, it will be very easy for the body to believe. That is because as soon as we say 'soul', we think of God. We think that inside the soul is God, or that inside God is the soul; the soul and God go together. God has given the message of the inner and outer running to the soul. Now the soul is trying to bring the younger members—the heart, mind, vital and body—along with it. But when the heart, mind and vital do not join with the soul, then suspicion starts in the physical consciousness.

If your goal is to run fifty miles per week, is it better to run seven miles a day or to vary the distance?

It is always good to have easy and hard days. It is best to have two easy days and then one hard day. Even having alternate easy and hard days is not good enough. If you run fifteen miles one day, it is not good to run seven or ten miles the next day. Instead, on your hard days cover twenty or twenty-five miles or even a full marathon. Then take two easy days. In this way, you can cover seventy or eighty miles a week.

Only those who are very strong and who are seriously training for long-distance running should do more than seventy miles a week. They can run one hundred miles or one hundred and twenty miles.

Sometimes when I start to run I get angry, even furious.

See if you have had enough rest. Perhaps you are compelling the body to run, but the body is not cooperating because you have not had sufficient sleep on those days. You have a very mild and kind nature, so I think that you are not getting enough rest at night. Then the following morning you curse yourself and ask yourself why you are running. You need more rest to calm your nerves.

How much weight training do we need to do to supplement our running?

Weightlifting twice a week is more than enough for a long-distance runner. Also, I do not advise any student of mine who is running long distances to practice lifting more than 30 pounds. Short-distance runners, sprinters, can go up to 50 pounds.

As a sprinter, what can I do to make my calves bigger? I have tried many things.

It is not the size but the strength that matters. There are many excellent sprinters who do not have big calf muscles, but still they have tremendous strength in their calves. Many runners and jumpers whose calf muscles are not so pronounced have enormous strength inside their calves. It is not the size but the strength inside the muscle that is needed.

How do you feel about bicycle training to improve running?

I did a great deal of bicycling when I lived in India in my youth. For at least two and a half hours every day I used to cycle as I did errands. It does not increase running speed at all, but something is better than nothing. Sometimes cycling can actually be a hindrance to running speed, because it develops special kinds of muscles which do not complement the speed muscles. Bicycling does help for endurance, but if you want to increase your running speed, then I do not advise it. You can cycle for endurance, or if you are injured and cannot run. For a little bit of stamina you can do it. But again, cycling stamina is totally different from running stamina. If one wants to become a good runner and maintain a five-minute pace, then cycling is not the answer. Quality road work is the answer.

> Yes, I can!
> I certainly can!
> I can succeed
> **Where nobody else**
> **Has dared to try.**

3
RACING

Imagination plays by far the greatest role
in increasing speed.

What should my attitude be when someone else wins a race I hoped to win?

As children, we learn how to walk only after repeated falls. We become good wrestlers by being defeated many times. We become the best runners after losing the race many times. If we feel sad when we observe someone else winning a race, this will not help us at all. But if we can appreciate the speed of the champion, automatically some of his capacity will enter into us. Through sincere appreciation we gain capacity. When I see that somebody is running the fastest, I really feel that I am that person. Similarly, if you can identify with other people's successes, instead of envying them, you will get a great deal more joy out of life. And, of course, if you can identify with their defeats as well, you will learn sympathy and kindness, as well as enriching your own experience.

> There are only three winners:
> The one who
>   Competes with himself,
> The one who
>   Crosses the finish line first
> And the one who
>   Finishes the race.

I find that during races my concentration varies a lot. Is there any way that I can maintain my concentration throughout the whole race?

This is my simple suggestion: before the competition starts, meditate most soulfully for five minutes. Try to make yourself feel that you are not the competitor, but that somebody else is running in and through you. You are only the witness, the spectator. Since somebody else is competing, you are at perfect liberty to watch and enjoy. While you are competing, sometimes it is very difficult to enjoy the race. Either the competitive spirit or frustration is killing you, or your body is not abiding by your mental will and you feel that you are literally dying. So many problems arise.

But before you start, if you can convince yourself that you are a divine observer and that somebody else is competing in you, through you and for you, then fear, doubt, frustration, anxiety and other negative forces will not be able to assail your mind. Once these thoughts occupy the mind, they try to enter into the vital and then into the physical. When they enter into the physical, they create tension, and this makes you lose all your power of concentration. But if you feel that you are not the competitor, if you feel that you are only observing the competition from the beginning to the end, then there will be no tension, and these forces will not attack you. This is the only way to overcome these forces and maintain the highest type of concentration from the beginning to the end.

This is what I do. As a runner I am useless, but right at the beginning I try to become an instrument and make myself feel that somebody else, my Beloved Supreme, is running in and through me. If I can offer my soulful gratitude to my Inner Pilot before the race and after the race also, then there can be no frustration, no decline of aspiration. The power of my concentration will remain the same throughout the race.

During training, an athlete sacrifices a great deal of time, and yet on the race day itself he may not be able to do well. What do you think is the attitude he should have towards this sort of thing?

It entirely depends on what kind of athlete one is. If one is a spiritual athlete, a seeker-athlete, then every day is a golden opportunity to become a better instrument of God; it is a lifelong process. If someone is not a seeker, but an ordinary athlete with abundant capacities, then he should feel that life is not a matter of self-giving or sacrifice. Life is only a matter of giving and taking.

When he is training, which means he is preparing himself, at that time he is giving. Then, on the particular day when there is an athletic meet, on that day he receives recognition. The athlete gives and gives and gives for a few months, and then there comes a time when he receives abundant appreciation, admiration and adoration. So how can there be any sacrifice? It is all give and take.

An athlete practises seriously for three or four months, and then during the competition he has to show his capacity. If he does poorly, he may think, "Oh, I made such sacrifices for so many months. Now what a deplorable result!" But it was not a sacrifice. He was only giving for a period of time, and now he is receiving the result in the form of an experience. The seeker who recognises his inner oneness with the rest of the world will not feel sad and miserable if he does poorly. Both success and failure are absolutely necessary for everybody in every walk of life.

> **The determination**
> **In your heroic effort**
> **Will permeate your mind and heart**
> **Even after your success or failure**
> **Is long forgotten.**

What role should competition play in one's running?

If the runner is not a seeker, his aim is immediate success and the immediate manifestation of his unparalleled supremacy. He wants to defeat all his rivals mercilessly and, like Julius Caesar, to declare, "I came, I saw, I conquered."

However if the runner is a seeker, then he has a special role. His role is to compete with himself and try to increase his own capacity. But he has to know that he will increase his capacity only by virtue of the infinite Grace of God, if so is the Will of God. So the seeker-runner will try to consciously surrender to the Will of God during his running career.

In the ordinary human life, we try to win by defeating others. In the spiritual life, we try to win by conquering the unaspiring and the undivine in ourselves.

> Competition is good,
> Provided it is the competition
> Of self-transcendence
> And not the competition
> Of ego-demonstration.

Is it better to concentrate or meditate when running a marathon?

It is always advisable to concentrate while running a marathon. If you meditate, then you will feel that you are either on the top of a snow-capped mountain or at the bottom of the sea. That is the very highest type of meditation, but it will not help your running. If you concentrate, on the other hand, then at every moment you will be able to regulate your steps and your forward movement. Also, discouraging, destructive and uncomely thoughts will not be able to lower your consciousness. If your consciousness is not lowered, then naturally you will run faster.

Before running, however, meditation is good to make the mind calm and quiet so that wrong forces do not enter. When you meditate, your mind acquires some poise. Then, while you are running, if you can bring forward this poise, it will help you overcome the mental frustration that often comes while running long distances. When you are running long distances, all kinds of frustrating thoughts can come and make you feel that what you are doing is useless. Or the mind will say, "Oh, this is boring," and you will not want to take one more step. But if you were able to meditate earlier in the day, then you will have acquired some solid inner strength that will carry you mile after mile. Also, meditation teaches you how to empty your mind of thoughts. And if you can keep thoughts out of your mind while you are running, it will help you tremendously—far beyond your imagination. At that time a new creation will be able to dawn inside you, and this will give you added inspiration and receptivity.

So while you are actually running, it is better to concentrate rather than meditate. Another thing you can do is inwardly sing spiritual songs soulfully and powerfully. This will also help keep your mind from becoming tired and frustrated and interfering with your running.

Why is a short race sometimes less comfortable than a long race?

In a short distance race, as soon as the gun is fired, you have to think of reaching the goal. But in a long-distance race, the goal remains for some time a far cry. During the time that it takes you to reach the goal, you can discover your own way to be physically more comfortable during the run. If you wish, you can go slowly and steadily like an Indian bullock cart. You can measure your distance mentally and calculate your capacities in your own way; you have the time. But for a short distance, in only a few fleeting seconds you have to reach the goal. You have to give your body, vital, mind, heart and soul most forcefully, if not willingly, to the goal. Therefore, it becomes most uncomfortable.

Before a 400-metre race, I am full of anxiety. I feel afraid of becoming too exhausted, even though I know from experience that this fear is baseless. Why am I so anxious?

For long-distance you need stamina and for short-distance you need speed. But the 400 metres demands both stamina and speed. So first of all, you should recognise that this is a most difficult race. But since you have run it many, many times, you know that you are not going to die. The difficulty, in your case, is not actually fear of exhaustion, but a subtle fear that you may not be first, which creates anxiety. You do not actually worry that after

400 metres you are going to collapse and die. That fear would be absolutely baseless. The real fear is that someone is going to beat you.

You have to learn the difference between anxiety and alertness. Anxiety and alertness are two different dynamic energies. With anxiety, you are always worrying about others and comparing yourself to them. But with alertness, you simply want to do the best you can. When the starter is about to fire the gun, you should be alert but not anxious.

Then, when the race starts, try to feel that you are the only runner in the race. Before the gun goes off, do not think of others; think only of yourself—that you are going to run at your own fastest speed. You want to see your capacity. Whether you come in first or last is for God to decide. So you will remain alert, but you will not think of others. In this way, there can be no anxiety.

In India I once saw a race among several men over the age of 65. Two of the runners had such false modesty that when the starter fired the gun they did not start. The starter said to one of the two men, "What are you doing?" The man said, "My friend has not yet started, so how can I start? It is not polite." He wanted to be such a perfect gentleman that he did not want to take any advantage!

When the starter said: "Go!" at that time it was for both of them. But this fellow looked to the side and, just because his friend had not started, he said, "How can I start now?" Everybody laughed and laughed while they were running. Naturally one of them was a better runner, but he did not want to stand first. He wanted to stay with the one who was lagging behind, so they ran side by side right to the finish line. Is it not the height of stupidity?

It is up to you to show your capacity. Whether you are going to come in first or last is for God to decide. You cannot say that you will not show your capacity just because somebody else will not be able to run as fast as you or will be able to run faster. Feel that you are the only runner, and you will run at your fastest speed. Before a race do not think of others; think only of yourself. Then there can be no anxiety.

> **He is really something!**
> **He always likes to compete with himself**
> **And transcend himself.**
> **God smiles with joy**
> **Because he competes with himself.**
> **God cries with joy**
> **Because he does really transcend himself.**

Recently, in a mile race, I ran the first two quarters on my pace, but in the third quarter my concentration went.

At that time, a kind of relaxation or complacent feeling came. You felt that you had already achieved your goal. You should have said to yourself, "I have achieved my goal for the first half, but I have another goal." If you always try to go beyond, to transcend, then you will have a better speed. Satisfaction is good, but it is also good to have hunger. If God gives you an iota of peace, you are satisfied, but you should want to have more peace. This hunger for something more we call receptivity. You can increase your receptivity. When you come to a particular standard, you have to say, "Is there anything more I can do?" Then do it.

If someone is near me, I find it easier to maintain the speed I want to maintain. But if no one is in front of me, I find it difficult to concentrate on speed.

At that time you have to use your stopwatch. If you know you can do under a five-minute pace for seven miles, then try to increase your capacity. You may be ahead of the other runners, but you are not ahead of your best possible time. Suppose you were planning to run at a 4:30 pace, but everyone is behind you, so you are not getting any inspiration or challenge. Just look at your stopwatch and think of it as another rival or competitor. Then you will be inspired to run faster.

What should we do when we feel like dropping out of a race?

We have to use our wisdom at every moment. Sometimes we are physically tired. Sometimes we are mentally tired. Sometimes we are emotionally tired. Sometimes we are tired without any rhyme or reason. Often our mental lethargy makes us feel that we will not be able to complete the race or, if we complete the race, nothing special is going to happen. There are so many ways in which our mind can convince us that it is useless and unnecessary to continue. The mind makes us feel, "I am just killing myself without any specific purpose."

If mental lethargy or our own unwillingness tortures us, we must not surrender to these wrong forces. Our motto is, "Never give up!" Only after we have given everything that we have and everything that we are can we give up if it is absolutely necessary. Otherwise, we are making the most deplorable mistake. Most of the time there is every possibility that we shall be able to arrive at our destination. And once we arrive at our destination, it is we who will be the happiest and the proudest person.

> **Failure-tears will always**
> **Remain as strangers**
> **To enthusiasm-smiles.**

Are love of sport and natural talent enough to win, or must an athlete develop a 'killer instinct'?

Natural talent and love of sport do help us considerably, but they are not enough. We need special Grace from God to be successful. Otherwise, many times various forces come and stand in our way, preventing us from being successful. So God's Grace is of paramount importance. God's Grace is like an unseen Hand, but when we get the result, it becomes seen and visible.

Suppose a race is very close and the capacity of two athletes is the same, but one of them is aspiring. Does God's Grace let the one who is aspiring win?

It depends on the Supreme's Will. If someone is very aspiring, the Supreme may tell the person, "All right, since you are sincerely dedicated to My Will, you do not have to win in the Olympics." Again, if someone is a seeker and he also has very great potential as an athlete, then the Supreme may give him just a little bit of success in sports.

> **In the inner and outer race,**
> **I will not say,**
> **"God wants me to win,"**
> **But**
> **"Let God's will be done."**

Does each individual have a predisposition for achieving greatness in one specific athletic event?

An individual athlete can easily shine in more than one athletic event. Right now Carl Lewis is the supreme athlete in the 100 metres, 200 metres, relay and the long jump. His idol-predecessor, Jesse Owens, was exceptional in the 100 metres, long jump and low hurdles. Again, decathlon champions like Bruce Jenner and Daley Thompson have excelled in ten different items. If an athlete has abundant receptivity, then he can receive divine inspiration and capacity from Above to offer seemingly miraculous results not only in various athletic fields but also in other fields as well

If we are running a race in New York and a great runner is running a world record on the other side of the world, does our aspiration or intensity help that other runner?

Definitely, provided that runner is also aspiring. It is like two individuals who are in the aspiration-boat together. Since you are in the same boat, your capacity, your intensity will enter into him and he will be able to go faster.

Is there a limit to any record?

There is only one limit: how much God wants to reveal Himself in and through each individual. The only limit is God's Will. God waits and waits and waits. Then, if He sees that somebody is receptive or that somebody has worked very hard, He may do something through that individual. Records will always be broken, but that does not mean that someone will be able to run one mile in a minute. But Bannister, Landy, Scott, Maree, Coghlan and all the great runners who are yet to come will go on breaking records, and the world will continue to progress.

> Impossible dreams are afraid of
> My sleepless and breathless
> Faith in God.

During the 21st century, will anybody break the two-hour marathon barrier?

How I wish the twenty-first century to prove my prophecy that someone will run a marathon in under two hours! I find it very difficult to believe that our human capacity is limited. Right now [1999] the world record for the marathon is 2:06. Just six minutes to reduce over twenty-six miles!

Unfortunately, human beings always think, "My capacity, my capacity." If the same world-class runners could say, "My capacity is coming from God. God is running in and through me," and really mean it, then you would see surprising results. There are at least twenty world-class marathon runners. If they could have that kind of faith, you would hear in one month that the world record has been smashed.

Unfortunately, athletes are not all seekers of the highest height. Otherwise, there is not a single record in the athletic world that cannot be smashed mercilessly—even the 100-metre sprint. To me, the present record for 100 metres is no record. They can easily bring it down to seven seconds. But who will believe me? Today I am a talker, but one day from Heaven, I will see that my prophecies have come true.

Everything is based on receptivity. In the weightlifting world, if I have to use my physical capacity without depending on God's unconditional Compassion and Grace, do you think I will be able to lift more than fifty pounds with one hand? I doubt it very much. Whether you believe me or say I am exaggerating my self-importance, I want to tell you that a maximum of sixty pounds I would be able to lift with each arm simultaneously. I am able to lift more only because I entirely depend on God's Grace.

When our receptivity increases, God increases our capacity. Before that, all the limitations of the body come and stay indefinitely because of our ingratitude-mind, ingratitude-heart and ingratitude-life. We have to feel that our capacity is coming from God. Why is it that one day you can get up early in the morning and another day you cannot? One day you are inspired; another day lethargy is absolutely killing you. For everything, we have to depend on God's Compassion. That does not mean we will just lie down, sleep and snore, and God will work. God does not want the surrender of an idle fellow. We shall pray to God for the fulfilment of His Will: "If such is Your Will, then use Your Capacity in and through me. I am doing this because I feel You are inspiring me to do it."

God has given each of us certain capacities. I may not be a runner, but somebody else may be a runner. I may be a singer, but somebody else may not be a singer. If anyone wants to increase his capacity in his own field, then he must have God-reliance, not self-reliance. Only then will his capacity become unlimited. Now our capacity is limited because we feel we are doing everything—we are taking this exercise and that exercise. We give ninety-nine per cent of the credit to what our mind is telling us and our life is prompting us to do. But if we can give one hundred per cent of the credit to God for whatever we are doing that is good and positive in our life, then our capacities will become unlimited.

It is all a question of receptivity. To be sincere, if I had to rely on my own capacity, I would be frightened to death to stand under the heavy weights that I lift. I would have all kinds of fears that something would break or something else would happen. In my case, it is only dependence, dependence—dependence on God's Grace. But again, I have to practise. I have to take this exercise and that exercise.

Now I have made a prophecy, and God alone knows when my prophecy will come true. The physical and the spiritual must go together. The physical is the temple and the spiritual is the shrine. They are both indispensable. How can there be a shrine if there is no temple? Will the wind not blow it away?

But when it comes to the marathon, my vision has not yet been manifested. So much depends on your inner happiness. You know how fast you achieve things on the days you are happy in comparison to other days. And the days when you have self-doubt, fear, jealousy and insecurity, you are ready to wait indefinitely to accomplish something or to come up to your own satisfactory standard.

What do you see in the future for long distance running?

In ten or twenty years, people will regard the marathon the way we regard a 10-mile race today. At that time they will consider 50 or 70 or 100 miles as long distance, and those kinds of races will be as popular as the marathon is today.

Now people are doing so well in the marathon. In a few years the best runners will run the marathon in under two hours. In twenty or thirty years people will run 50 or 100 miles at a five-minute pace. The children of people who are running the marathon now will run at the present marathon pace for 30 or 40 miles, and then even farther. They will have such stamina!

> **My heart runs**
> **The world's longest race**
> **And not my mind.**
> **My Lord runs ahead of me;**
> **My breath runs behind.**

Recently sports writers have been talking about a feeling in all kinds of athletes where everything slows down. What is it all about?

It is like smooth sailing. In the beginning, all kinds of personal effort are necessary. For years an athlete may work very, very hard, with tremendous intensity. Then, during his race, he feels that he is not moving at all; but actually he *is* moving—like smooth sailing. At that time, he is not the doer. Somebody else is doing it in and through him.

When Bill Rodgers is running a marathon well, he is coasting. He may be running for 26 miles, but he is maintaining the same speed or even increasing the speed, but with no effort.

When you start a machine, you hear all kinds of noises. It takes time to warm up. But once the machine is operating at full speed, you do not hear those same noises. That is like coasting in marathon running. At the beginning of the race so much effort is required, but then, when it becomes smooth sailing, sometimes you do not appreciate it because you have the feeling that you are doing nothing.

At that time God's Grace has descended and God has added something new to your capacity. Then you will offer God your tears of gratitude. Receptivity increases only in one way: by increasing our gratitude to God.*

> Our heart's gratitude
> Produces a sleepless energy
> Which helps us bring about success
> In each and every aspect of our life.

Does the triathlon have any spiritual or symbolic significance?

Swimming reminds us of our spiritual life. Right now we are swimming in the sea of ignorance, but we are praying to our Beloved Supreme and meditating on Him to be able to swim in the sea of Light and Delight. Swimming has its own symbolic value. I always say that we are sailing in the Golden Boat with the Golden Boatman towards the Golden Shore. The spiritual significance of water is consciousness. We are all eager to be in a good consciousness. As soon as we are in water, consciousness enters. So swimming has its own very special reality and divinity. While we are swimming, we can imagine that we are crossing from ignorance-sea into the sea of light and wisdom.

While we are cycling, we are reminding ourselves of evolution, of how the world is evolving in cycles. When we think of our planet, we think of a wheel turning. Our life also is evolving like a wheel. So cycling reminds us of the process of evolution

---

*Sri Chinmoy has recommended offering gratitude to God after completing each mile of a marathon.

and of how everything goes in cycles. Once upon a time, in the hoary past, we lived in an era of truth. Now we are living in an era of falsehood. There was a time when truth reigned supreme, but now we see at every moment and every place that falsehood is reigning supreme. Our goal is to bring back again the Golden Age in which truth will be our inner guide and reign supreme.

Running, as I have said, reminds us of our birthless and deathless journey along Eternity's Road.

I appreciate and admire the athletes who have tremendous capacity in these three major events: swimming, cycling and running. Each event is so significant. We want to swim in the sea of Light and Delight and not in the sea of ignorance-night. We are running along Eternity's Road. And in the process of evolution, our life-process, our life-energy is spinning so fast. The faster we can go, the sooner we will be able to have outer success and inner progress. And with our outer success and inner progress, we will be able to arrive at our Goal infinitely faster than otherwise.

As a meditation teacher, why do you encourage your students to organise races?

I encourage and inspire my students to organise and participate in triathlons, long-distance races and short-distance races precisely because I feel that the world needs dynamism. The outer world needs dynamism and the inner world needs peace. We are all seekers; so we pray and meditate in order to have peace. Again, we feel that if we can be dynamic, then we will be able to accomplish much in our outer life. To be dynamic we need physical fitness at every moment, and running helps us considerably to keep physically fit. Running is helping and inspiring people considerably, and in our races we have been inspiring thousands of people all over the world.

What do your multi-day races contribute to the world?

Athletes derive tremendous benefit from these multi-day races. They go beyond their capacities. In order to be happy, we have to go always beyond and beyond and beyond our capacities. So here, while running, each runner is getting a very special opportunity to go beyond his or her capacities. Self-transcendence is the only thing a human being needs in order to be truly happy. So these races help the runners tremendously, although outwardly they go through such hardship. Eventually, when the race is over, they feel they have accomplished something most significant.

Any extraordinary activity we perform on earth in the outer world—whether it is a long-distance run or a short-distance run, or jumping or throwing—shows that in the inner world that capacity *does* exist. It is only that we have to use it. The capacity that we appreciate, admire and adore on earth can be seen, felt and acquired in the inner world in infinitely greater measure.

The inspiration that we give to the outer world by exercising our extraordinary capacity comes from the ever-mounting aspiration of the inner world. Our achievements add to the receptivity of the outer world, to make the outer world eventually ready to accept the inner capacities of love, peace and bliss in infinite measure.

Human pride has to be devoured for the development of humility, which we all desperately need to make inner and outer spiritual progress. It is our spiritual progress which will make us God-champions in each and every field of life. Again, there is something called divine pride. This divine pride breathlessly whispers in our ears: "You are the choicest instrument of God. It is beneath your dignity to wallow in the pleasures of ignorance-night. God wants you to be an exact prototype of His universal manifestation and transcendental Dream." So this divine pride I have seen and felt in each of the ultrarunners. I have seen and felt God's own Pride, founded upon His infinite Delight in each of them.

> The pride of the earthly race
> And the joy of the Heavenly Race
> Have the same goal:
> Self-transcendence.

Why is long-distance running becoming more popular in America these days [1980s]?

Previously America's soul cared only for speed. Like a bullet, America wanted to run faster than the fastest, and it showed only its speed. Everything it did was faster than the fastest. But when it was a matter of endurance, America became frightened. American speed and American endurance did not rhyme in those days. But now America feels that speed is necessary and endurance is also necessary. So now America cares for speed and it also cares for stamina.

Whenever America takes up something, it is only a matter of time before it does that thing well. Now that America has accepted long-distance running, it has improved tremendously in this area. How many excellent, super-excellent long-distance runners America has already produced, although long-distance running has been part of the American consciousness only for the last few years. Frank Shorter, Bill Rodgers and so many others have immortalised long-distance running in the consciousness of America in a few short years. When the consciousness of a country accepts a particular thing, that is the golden time. Ten or twelve years ago it was all short-distance running. But now is the golden time, the opportune time, for long-distance running in America. Several years ago, who cared for 24-hour races or 50-mile and 70-mile races? Even in the newspaper, one rarely saw anything about ultramarathons. The ultramarathon almost did not exist. But now it is common. All over the world, in fact, there is such interest in long-distance running, specially marathons.

Long-distance running gives us a real feeling of accomplishment. We can run 100 metres forty times during the year and not feel the same sense of accomplishment as when we run one marathon. But speed and endurance are both important, specially in the spiritual life. If one has only speed, then one cannot ultimately succeed; we need endurance because the goal is quite far. Again, if one has only stamina and no speed, then it will take forever to reach the goal. Only if someone has both qualities will he be able to make very good progress in his spiritual life and achieve something really great in life.

What do you feel about children running long-distance races?

It is my inner feeling, my spiritual, yogic feeling, that it is not at all good for children to run long-distance; it is not good for their growth. An Indian child should not run more than one mile if he is under thirteen years of age. But for Americans, I would put the age at ten years. Children under ten should not run more than a mile. If they want to run three miles, they should be at least thirteen years of age.

These children will live on earth for many years. Right now let them do sprinting. Let them do 50, 60 or 200 metres; let them do 400 metres or 800 metres maximum. But children's lung capacity and heart condition may not be strong enough for long-distance running—specially children who are in their formative years. Perhaps doctors will say that long-distance running is good for children, but I feel it may lead to some serious problems and is very dangerous.

I feel very sad that parents are not wise in this matter. They are doing an injustice to their children. A seed germinates, and then it becomes a plant. If you speed up its growth unnaturally, it may grow a little taller. But if you raise it too high, there will be no roots there. It will not be able to grow into a normal, natural tree.

The loser's inner speed
Is lethargy.
The loser's outer speed
Is unwillingness.

The winner's inner speed
Is self-offering.
The winner's outer speed
Is self-perfection-smile.

4
FATIGUE AND INJURIES

Physical energy has only one source,
and that source is spiritual energy.

I find that sometimes I go through a period of making very good progress in running. I am increasing my mileage, feeling great, getting good speed. And then after some time everything falls apart and my running goes downhill.

It happens to everyone. Life goes up and down. The main thing is to get satisfaction. When you are unable to reach your peak, you should not feel that it is your fault. It is not that you have deliberately injured yourself. If you are deliberately enjoying your lack of speed or lack of enthusiasm, then you are to be blamed. But if circumstances have led you to this condition, please try to maintain your equanimity and peace of mind. Feel that you are going through a phase that may last for three or four weeks, but that eventually it will pass.

Try to think of the summit which you reached two or three weeks earlier, and try to remember the joy that you felt. Then you will see that the joy you got from your previous achievements will carry you through, and very soon you will not only reach but transcend your previous height. You are not fooling yourself; you are only bringing happiness into your system, and this happiness is confidence. Again, confidence itself is happiness.

Try to feel that your problem is just a small obstacle, a hurdle that you will soon overcome. Then you will be able to diminish the frustration that you now feel. But if you maintain or increase your frustration, then the problem will linger.

These downhill periods happen to everyone. Is there any runner who can say that he has never had any difficulties? Only for short-distance runners is it possible to maintain their performance. If they are not injured, then for months and months they can keep the same speed. But for long-distance runners it is not possible.

How would you describe it when someone "hits the wall" during a marathon?

It means that your exhaustion has touched its ultimate height. When you reach this point, everything may go blank before your eyes or you may see all black. You might feel that there is a thick wall right in front of you that you cannot penetrate, or a vast ocean or a big mountain that will not allow you to go further. It is an obstacle that you cannot go beyond.

Hitting the wall is the feeling that all your life-energy has deserted you. It means that you have an absolutely real sense of collapse. Your body gives you the feeling that death is imminent. At that time, real discouragement—physical, vital and mental—assails your life. When you really hit the wall, all your strength and determination desert you.

How can we effectively channel physical energy into spiritual energy?

We have to know that physical energy has only one source, and that source is spiritual energy. As long as we remain in the body-consciousness, we are not aware of this. But when we go deep within, we see that spiritual energy is the source of physical, vital and mental energy. When spiritual energy enters into the physical, it is unable to maintain its pristine purity. What we need is purity in the inner plane and dedication on the outer plane. Then spiritual energy enters into physical energy, and physical energy becomes an added strength to spiritual energy.

Do people really need more sleep when they are training for athletics?

For spiritual people, specially advanced seekers, it is not necessary. By drawing down cosmic energy, in two minutes they can get the rest of two hours, three hours, four hours. It depends on how effectively you can draw in the cosmic energy. But runners who are not spiritual seekers do have to sleep longer.

How can we conquer laziness and be more active, specially in the morning?

Early in the morning, try to get up at 5:30 and feel that if you run or take some other exercise, this is as important as your meditation. If you feel that meditation is infinitely more important than your exercises, then you are wrong. Inside your physical exercise you will find the capacity and the necessity of your meditation. True, meditation will take you to God-realisation, whereas physical exercise will not. But physical exercise will definitely help you energise your body, and you will have a very sound, deep and sublime meditation.

So early in the morning, take some exercise and feel that this is going to add to your meditation. Then laziness will disappear in the morning.

> **The morning hope-beauty blesses**
> **The morning runners.**
> **The evening peace-fragrance blesses**
> **The evening runners.**

Should we run even when we are extremely tired?

As a rule, when we are extremely tired, it is not advisable to run, for it will not help us in any way. At that time, running will be nothing but fatigue and self-destruction, and it will leave in our mind a bitter taste. But sometimes, even when we are not physically tired, we feel that we are. We are only mentally tired or emotionally tired, but the mind convinces us that we are physically tired. Our human lethargy is so clever! It acts like a rogue, a perfect rogue, and we get tremendous joy by offering compassion to our body. We offer all kinds of justifications for the body's lethargy and make ourselves feel that the body deserves rest.

So we have to be sincere to ourselves. If we really feel extremely tired, then we should not run. But we have to make sure that it is not our lethargic mind, our lethargic vital or our lethargic physical consciousness that is making us feel that we are extremely tired. This kind of tricky cleverness we have to conquer.

With our imagination-power we can challenge the tricky mind and win. We weaken ourselves by imagining that we are weak. Again, we can strengthen ourselves by imagining that we are strong. Our imagination often compels us to think we cannot do something or cannot say something. We often use imagination in a wrong direction. So instead of letting imagination take us backwards, we should use it to take us forward towards our goal.

How can we keep going in the seven-day race?

Please do not think of all seven days while you are running. Think of only one day at a time. Then, do not even think of one day; think of only seven hours. Then, for a few minutes, think of only one hour. If you can mentally divide the race and break it down into separate parts, you will get much more energy and much more joy while running. Every time your mind decreases the amount of time you have to run, you will get tremendous inner strength and vigour. So do not keep in mind seven days. Go at your own pace, but mentally divide the race to make the distance as short as possible. In this way, you will always have inner strength and be able to run throughout.

> Run!
> You can easily challenge
> The pride of frightening distance.

How can I quickly regain my inner and outer strength after a multi-day race?

Eat voraciously, and do not worry about your weight! No matter how much you weigh, you are not going to be fat. Eat, eat, eat! And while eating, remain happy, happy, happy. You are eating earthly, material food, but feel the divine joy in it. Then also feel gratitude inside your heart that God chose you to accomplish this great feat. Your cheerful gratitude will strengthen your body far beyond your imagination.

How do you run through inner pain?

Inner pain is a joke. Outer pain I believe in. Sometimes I cannot place my foot on the ground without getting such pain! But inner pain—which comes from frustration, depression, jealousy and insecurity—is a joke. Inner pain should be discarded like a filthy rag! Outer pain you cannot so easily ignore, but inner pain must be discarded.

If you have inner pain, if you are jealous of someone let us say, then the outer running will actually help you. When you are running and perspiring, when you are struggling, at that time the inner pain goes away to some extent. Otherwise, if you do not go out to run because you are depressed, then you are just a fool.

If you feel depressed while you are running, you can sing loudly and deliberately try to sing wrong notes. Then laugh at yourself. Some of my friends used to do this. They were good singers, but deliberately they would sing wrong notes while they were walking, and it would make them laugh. In that way they got rid of depression.

> Fear is a limping thought.
> Doubt is a blinding thought.
> Courage is a galloping thought.
> Faith is an illumining thought.

Why do we get injuries for no apparent reason?

There is always a reason, either in the inner world or in the outer world. In the inner world, if something is dislocated—if your consciousness has descended or if some hostile forces have attacked—you get an injury. Again, sometimes you are totally innocent, but the wrong forces, the malicious forces which are hovering around, can cause injury.

So, in the inner world either your consciousness has descended because of wrong thoughts, or some hostile force has attacked you, and that is why you get an injury which you cannot see any reason for.

Always when I become very interested in the physical and in playing sports, I injure myself to the point where I have to stop completely. Why does this happen?

What actually happens in your case is that when you enter into the physical world—playing tennis or running—you do not give value to the physical as such. You remain in the mind. A portion of your existence you throw into the game and another portion you keep totally in the mind-world. It is like cutting yourself in half. You are keeping your body on the first floor, but your consciousness is always on the upper floor, in the mind. If you can direct more of your mental energy into the physical when you play, this will not happen.

You want to play; you want to win. But actually the concentration of the mind, the real concentration, is not in the physical itself. You know that you are playing tennis, but the concentration that the body needs from the mind is not there. The body is helpless without concentration from the mind. So when you play, do not think of your mental work. Because there is a gap between your mind's concentration and your physical activity, you may have unfortunate experiences in life.

If one is in generally good health, what would cause pain and aches in the body?

It is one thing to have good health and another thing to deliberately maintain good health. It is like having a large amount of money without knowing about it. If you are not conscious of it, you may easily lose it. You may have good physical health, but perhaps in two months' time you have not thought of your body once, let alone tried to increase the strength of your legs or arms.

If you are aware of something, immediately it shines and gets a new luminosity. By giving attention to something, you give new life to it. If you consciously maintain good health, your body gets new life.

How can we spiritually heal injuries?

It is a matter of inner capacity. One kind of capacity is to heal the injury by bringing down peace and light from Above. Another kind of capacity is to ignore the pain altogether. During your meditation, if all of a sudden you have intense aspiration, then you can bring down more light from Above to cure your injury. But you have to do this consciously during your meditation. If during the day you casually say, "Oh, how I wish I did not have any pain!" that will be useless. But while you are meditating, if you suddenly remember your pain, that is the time to pray and bring down more light.

Again, you can increase your capacity to tolerate pain. If you had had the same kind of pain four years ago perhaps you would not have been able to run. If it is bearable, try to run according to your own capacity. At that time, do not think of how fast this person or that person is running. Just go according to your own capacity and remain cheerful.

But sometimes the pain is unbearable and it is absolutely impossible to run. Then what can you do? If it is beyond your capacity to ignore the pain, in addition to praying and meditating, you can also go to the outer doctor. Light is also inside the doctor. But in some cases there is no way to cure the pain.

When I run I sometimes get a slight knee pain. Should I stop running at that time?

If you get just a slight pain in your knee, and if the pain is bearable, then you should continue running. At that time, feel that if you run a hundred metres more, the pain will go away. Then, after you have covered a hundred metres, feel that the pain will definitely stop if you run another hundred metres. If you do this five or six times, then most of the pain will go away. Even if some pain remains, the mind has already taken away your awareness from it. Your mind has forgotten about it. But if the pain is absolutely unbearable, what can you do? You simply have to surrender to it and stop running, at least for a while.

Sometimes I feel pain in my foot, and I start worrying that if I keep running, I might get a stress fracture. This happens even if the pain is not that bad and I know that probably nothing will happen.

If it is unbearable, excruciating pain, then something serious might happen. But if there is just a tiny pain in your foot, this kind of fear is only false anxiety that is coming to your mind. If you are worried, you can take rest for a few days and see if the pain goes away. If it leaves in just a day or two, you will know that it was nothing serious. In this way, you will become more confident that nothing will happen to your foot if you run.

So if the pain is not that serious, you do not have to worry. Your foot is not going to give out. It is only that fear has entered into your mind, and the mind has created false anxiety in you, a false alarm. You should not cherish these fears.

Can you get rid of an injury by lifting weights?

Many people are of the opinion that if you use very light weights and do lots of repetitions, then slowly and steadily you can strengthen your muscles and nerves and eventually get rid of an injury. Unfortunately, this is not my personal experience. I do not think my weightlifting will take away my pain. My physical pain, specially my knee pain, will go away only by the infinite Grace of my Beloved Supreme.

If you have a sports injury, for example, a calf injury, is there any way to inwardly heal it totally?

Everything has to depend on prayer and meditation. Again, outer therapy is also of supreme necessity. Then, if you can take minor stretching exercises to strengthen the calf, it may help. But if the exercises create more pain for you, then I advise you to go to a therapist.

Of course, the most important thing is the inner prayer. But it is like a boxer using two hands. With one hand you cannot do everything. God created medical science. You should take as much help from medical science as possible and, at the same time you have to think of our spiritual science, which is prayer and meditation. They have to go side by side. Since we are spiritual people, we have to give preference to the aspiration-aspect of life and, at the same time, we have to give considerable importance to medical science. God is also operating in and through medical science.

> **Each new start**
> **Strengthens my determination**
> **And**
> **Lengthens my aspiration.**
> **Believe it or not!**

5
MASTERS-CATEGORY RUNNERS

*If you want to make the fastest progress,
you have to have a childlike heart.*

At the opening of the 5th World Masters Games, held in San Juan, Puerto Rico, in September 1983, Sri Chinmoy offered the following remarks:

These Masters Games offer us a special message. They make us feel that even though we may be forty, fifty, sixty, seventy, eighty or even ninety years old, we are still God's children. When someone is fifty years old, it is very difficult for him to think of himself as a child. For us to think of ourselves as children is very difficult because we have developed the mind. But the Masters Games help us feel that we are truly children, for it is only children who like to play. People who are advanced in years will stay home and watch television or read newspapers, but children have boundless energy. They have hope, they have ambition, they have determination. They want to become good, better, best.

Most of the time, elderly people feel that they are finished products, that their life is over. So they do not have any hope or promise. But the Masters Games show us that elderly people can have hope and promise. It shows that elderly people can become inseparably one with children, with the new generation.

We are here at the Masters Games to make ourselves feel that we are children—God's children. For it is only children who have higher goals and make progress. Old people have given up their goals and are only waiting for death's hour to strike. But the people who are participating in these Games are telling death, "We are not ready for you, for we have still many things to accomplish here on earth. You are knocking at our door at the wrong time!"

Do you feel the World Masters Games will ever become as popular as the Olympics?

There is every possibility that the World Masters Games will become very popular in terms of bringing real joy to mankind. In the Olympics, each individual is trying to win a gold medal. But the real meaning behind the gold medal is joy. A grandfather may not bring back a gold medal but he brings back joy. He comes all the way from an obscure village to compete and, when he goes back home, his grandchildren are not going to ask him, "Can you show me your gold medal?" No, the fact that he has received such joy from competing is enough. This grandfather perhaps for many months did not smile; he was thinking of his sport or collecting money to come to Puerto Rico. But now the whole family is seeing that the grandfather is so happy. If the father sees that the son has become an Olympian, he will be so proud. Similarly, if the son sees that the father has received real joy by participating in these Masters Games, it will be a happy family. One individual has come from an Indian village and another has come from an Australian village. When they go back to their countries and speak to their children, grandchildren, friends and neighbours about the Games, and when others see such joy in them, then this joy will spread like wildfire in their village, town, city and country.

So it is quite possible that eventually the Masters Games will be as popular or even more popular than the Olympics. Most of the athletes are not expecting to break any record; they are happy just to participate and get innocent joy. But many Olympic athletes will go home feeling really miserable because they had come for a gold medal and perhaps did not even get the bronze. But in the Masters Games, even if your place is last, you are very happy.

It is like the difference between amateurs and professionals. In tennis, for example, as soon as people become good players, they turn professional so that they can become millionaires overnight. Then the real joy goes away from the game. In the Olympics, the athletes are not getting money; they are just getting gold medals. But still, much of the joy has disappeared from the competition. So many people are looking for name and fame for their countries, and the prestige of all the countries is at stake. The countries spend thousands and thousands of dollars on the athletes, and there are so many businesses that act as sponsors. But in the Masters Games, everybody comes at their own expense just for the joy of competing. If they can continue like this—doing everything at their own expense—then they will continue getting pure joy and giving pure joy to mankind.

The world is crying for joy, and I think the Masters Games will give more joy than the Olympics because the competition is not on such a vital plane. Here, in the competition there is a psychic touch. People have become more mature over the years; they have gone through success and failure many, many times. When they were young, almost all of them had the same kind of qualities that the young ones have today. But now that they are older, they do not want to manifest those qualities. They are looking only to give and receive joy. Here you have people from various countries coming together and making friends. If I come here and make a friend, and if we both become friends with someone else, then how can there ever be any conflicts in the world? These types of games give us a golden opportunity to become one family, and they contribute tremendously to the joy of the world-family.

Sri Chinmoy made the following remarks in Sacramento, California, on 1 June 1996 after competing in the California Senior Games.

The younger you can become, the faster will be your progress. This is absolutely no joke! I am fast approaching sixty-five years of age. I shall do a few more things in this lifetime which I could not do in my adolescent years. I have already done the head balance, which I could never do, even when I was a champion athlete. And there are five or six more things I shall do in this incarnation which, at the time of my athletic career, I could not do.

If you want to make the fastest progress, you have to have a childlike heart. Feel that you are only seven years old. It is the mind that makes us feel we are too old, we are useless, we can do nothing. This mind has to be silenced by the will of the heart, by the will of the soul. Age is in the mind; age is not in the body. When we think that we are old, that is the end, the very end, of our journey.

Even if you do not want to take exercise early in the morning, try to make yourself feel that you are quite young. Just go outside and see what happens. Then, while you are walking, try to walk a little faster. While you are doing anything, make the movement faster. Bring back your childlike days when you used to run and play with utmost joy.

>   Running makes the body young.
>   Striving makes the vital young.
>   Smiling makes the mind young.
>   Serving makes the heart young.
>   Loving makes the soul young.

Can you tell us something about your experience while you participated in these Senior Games?

Here there is no competitive spirit. Here there is no greed involved. Here there is only joy. It is through joy that we are going to transcend ourselves.

It is quite natural for a teenager to run. But at the age of sixty-five if I run, it means I am trying to maintain some joy, some enthusiasm. I am also trying to keep my body fit. When we are young, running is all competition; we want to defeat everybody and become the winner. Here the philosophy is totally different. If we can have cheerfulness and happiness, then that is our best achievement. At this age to do anything happily, cheerfully and self-givingly is most difficult.

Here I am competing with myself in order to maintain my inner joy and outer joy. When I run, I try my best to bring forward the enthusiasm that I had when I was a teenager. I try my best, but most of the time it does not come. The lethargy of the body does not allow me to bring forward the same quickness, alertness and promptness. I am imagining something, but the reality is somewhere else. When I was young, I did not have to imagine anything. I only used my capacity, which became reality. At that time, reality was pushing me forward. Now imagination is desperately trying to push me forward.

Our philosophy is the philosophy of self-transcendence. No matter how old we are, we are trying to increase our capacities and transcend our achievements.

> Yes, I can!
> I certainly can!
> I can become
> An impossibility-challenger
> In my inner life
> And in my outer life.

Why is the development of the Senior Olympics important?

I am very happy because those who participate in the Senior Olympics are utilising time in a divine way. There are two kinds of time. One is fleeting time. Another is eternal Time. Here these people who are advanced in life are trying to defy the attacks of self-doubt, frustration, failure and so many negative things. As we advance in age, incapacity lords it over us. We can no longer do this, we can no longer do that. Ten years ago we did it, but now we cannot run fast, we are unable to do so many things. Then we become frustrated.

But the Senior Olympians are saying, "No! We are still walking along the same road. Sometimes we are sprinting, sometimes we are running, sometimes we are jogging, and sometimes we are crawling. But as long as we keep to the same road, we will reach the destination." We often see a marathon runner running very fast. Then, towards the end of the race, how difficult it is for him to run! He is obliged to walk. Finally, when he reaches his destination at the end of 26 miles, he gets tremendous joy. So here also the Senior Olympians, after the age of 55, may not run as fast as they did in their prime. But the fact that they are still willing to run and eager to run deserves tremendous appreciation and admiration from us.

Is there any age limit to running?

There is no age limit; age surrenders. When we pray and meditate, we go far beyond the domain of the mind, the physical mind that doubts our capacities. When we pray and meditate, we identify ourselves with something vast and infinite. So there is no age limit, but we have to go far beyond the domain of the physical mind which binds us and discourages us at every moment. It says, "You cannot do this, you cannot do that, it is not possible for you." But when we pray and meditate, when we live in the heart, there is no such thing as impossibility.

> **You can enjoy a limitless life of glory**
> **If you do not allow**
> **Your life to be bound**
> **By your body's rules and regulations.**

Sri Chinmoy and Carl Lewis enjoy a ceremonial 100m run to inaugurate the Sri Chinmoy Peace Track at the University of Houston, where Carl Lewis was training at the time (17 October 1992).

6
ADVICE TO CARL LEWIS

Feel that God Himself, your Beloved Supreme,
is running in and through you.

Carl Lewis: How should I pray when I'm preparing for competition, during the practice time and also right before a race?

We use the term 'Supreme' as a synonym for God. If you can pray to the Supreme with an eagerness to please Him and fulfil Him, then he will run the race in and through you and also for you. Always feel that you are running not for yourself but for Him—only to please Him.

If you try to please only yourself, today you will be very happy that you are the world champion in the 100 metres. But tomorrow you may pray to God to reduce your timing—to run the 100 metres in eight seconds. The day after tomorrow you may ask God to grant you the ability to run it in seven seconds. In this way your demands may never end. At the same time, you will always be thinking of somebody who may defeat you. There will be a sense of insecurity or insufficiency. You will never feel complete.

But when you pray to God to fulfil Himself in and through you, you will be the happiest person no matter what you achieve, because God will give you His own Happiness. Only when we please God in His own Way can we become really happy.

When you pray, feel that you are an instrument. Feel that God Himself, your Beloved Supreme, is running in and through you. Then it is His responsibility to make you the happiest person in His own Way—by making you first or last. It will not matter to you whether you finish a few metres ahead of someone or a few metres behind someone. You will be happy because you are fulfilling God's Will.

Humanity received absolutely the highest prayer from the Saviour Christ when he said, "Let Thy Will be done." Indian spiritual Masters of the highest order have also said the same thing: "Lord Supreme, do execute Your Will in and through me."

Now you are happy because you are the fastest runner in the outer world. But when you become the fastest runner, the supreme hero, in the inner world, the joy that you get is infinite.

At that time you become the happiest person by becoming one with your own infinite Light and Delight. When this happens, the outer happiness that you previously felt fades into insignificance.

> Try to move forward
> Out of the aspiration-blocks
> As powerfully as possible
> If you want your life
> To breast victory's tape
> As quickly as possible.

Advice for the 1984 Olympics

Sri Chinmoy sent this message to Carl Lewis on 18 February 1984, at a time the champion athlete was experiencing some difficulties in his indoor competitions.

For the past few weeks, in the 50 metres and 60 metres you have been coming in second.

For us, the thought of your being second in this event is far beyond our imagination. But to me the 50-metre and 60-metre races are of no importance at all. When the world speaks of sprinting or the fastest sprinter, it speaks of the 100 metres. When we talk about Jesse Owens being the fastest runner, we never think of 50 yards or 50 metres or 60 metres; we think only of 100 metres. Go to any obscure country and ask who is the fastest. Immediately they will say the name of the person who is first in 100 metres. In this respect, your name has covered the length and breadth of the world. The whole world knows you as the best, the superlative sprinter.

When I came to America and heard about 40, 50 and 60-metre races, it amused me more than it inspired me. If people want to value only the shortest distance, then there will have to be a

10-metre or a 2-metre race. Or some silly people will say that whoever comes out of the starting blocks first is the fastest sprinter. But if this person has to run 70 or 80 or 100 metres, perhaps he will be nowhere. Some runners are still behind even up to the 90-metre mark. But when it is 100 metres, they defeat their rivals.

So please feel that 100 metres is the real race—not 60 metres or 10 metres or 2 metres! Please concentrate only on your 100 metres. Let the world mock you. As you have something to do, the world also has something to do. Let the world say whatever it wants to say or feel whatever it wants to feel. If you have already decided not to do any more short distances before the Olympics, then do not surrender your adamantine will to public criticism. People may try to instigate you to run more short distances, but if you have already decided not to run anymore, do not surrender to their unforgivable instigation.

If you want to continue and say, "I shall accept the challenge! I want to prove that I can do it," then that is another matter. But the only thing is, the Olympics are fast approaching, and I personally feel that the time has come for you to concentrate on the 100 and 200 metres and on the long jump. Who knows, perhaps God is giving the runners who are right now defeating you in shorter distances just a few drops of Nectar, whereas He has decided to give you a very large quantity at a later time. Or perhaps He is giving them some crumbs and plans to give you a big loaf. Anyway, you please make your decision. If you feel it is inadvisable to run the shorter distances, then do not listen to the critics.

In case you are tempted to do 50 or 60 metres, I wish to offer you some advice on a very practical level. Of course, being a spiritual man, everything I say comes from a spiritual plane. When running 50 or 60 metres in competition, before the starter fires the gun please try to feel that you have to run 10 metres less than the other competitors. If the race is 50 metres, then convince yourself that you are running 40 metres. If it is 60 metres, make yourself feel that you are going to do 50. If you feel that they have to run 10 metres farther to reach the goal, then naturally you will feel that you will win. When you feel that your task is easier than their task, you will get an extra surge of joy—we use the spiritual term 'delight'—that will help you succeed. You will have a very strong, cheerful, inner frame of mind and be able to run much faster. Then, by God's Grace you will be able to always do a miracle on the track.

But even though you make yourself feel that you are running a shorter distance than your rivals, you will not come to an absolute halt after you have covered that distance. In the 100 metres, for example, everybody advises the runners to maintain their speed even after they have passed through the tape. That is absolutely the right thing to do. Similarly, if you convince yourself that you are running only 50 metres whereas your rivals are running 60 metres, after 50 metres you cannot let your speed drop. You have to continue your speed right to the end.

Also, while you are running, try to feel that you are being chased rather than being pulled by something or someone. That way you will go faster. If somebody is chasing you, your speed will be faster than if somebody in front of you is pulling you towards him with a rope. If you feel that a magnet is pulling you to the finish line, you will run fast; but you will run faster if you feel that somebody is chasing you and you are running for your life. Imagine that a ferocious tiger is right behind you and at any moment is going to devour you. You know how fast a tiger can run! So you will run for your most precious life, and you will run the fastest. If the image of a tiger is not pleasing to your mind or heart, then think that your house has caught fire and you are running to the nearest telephone booth to call the fire department. When you see that your most valuable house is being burned to ashes, definitely you will run the fastest.

If you cannot think of a tiger or a fire, then try to feel that you are one or two metres ahead of everyone else right from the beginning. Before the race has started even, when you are taking the set position at the starting blocks, please try to feel that the other five or six runners are behind you. Then, when you start, feel that they are not running with you but are chasing you because you are trying to eat something most delicious and they want to deprive you of it. If you can feel that your rivals are behind you, chasing you, then you will be able to run much faster than if you see that the others are all on a line with you. So if you can feel that your competitors are a little behind and chasing you, and that you are running for your life, this will give you more inner intensity and outer determination. All this that I am saying also applies to the 100 metres.

About your long jump, people are enjoying a kind of malicious pleasure and accusing you of taking drugs, which is totally false, absolutely false! Unthinkable criticism has always been the order of the day, and there are always people who will say things that have no foundation. On the one hand, you have accepted the challenge and are doing absolutely the right thing. On the other hand, if you have to prove yourself to others in this way, then you are just surrendering to their whims. Today you have accepted this challenge.

Tomorrow they may say something else very painful about your running and jumping, and again you will have to prove that they are wrong. Instead of proving to them that they are wrong, just think of your promise to the world at large that you will do something incredible. Only dream of those incredible things and do not surrender to the stupid criticism of humanity. In the future, if they bring up the same stupid subject, please do not listen to them!

Now I am giving you some suggestions on the practical plane for the Olympics. When you start the long jump, please try to run for the full length; do not shorten your distance. It is absolutely important to have your proper distance. When you are about to start, of course you will pray and meditate the way you have been doing. But at the same time, try to feel that you are hearing people repeating your name: "Carl Lewis, Carl Lewis, Carl Lewis." Like a thunderous noise, most powerfully, feel that you are hearing your name repeated.

Another thing: when you are about to start, try to feel that you are representing not only America but all of earth. Feel that a competition is going on between earth and Heaven. Since you took birth on earth, you are representing earth and demonstrating earth's capacity to the Cosmic Gods and Goddesses. Try to feel that the whole earth is behind you and that you are getting blessings, love, concern, determination and oneness from the entire earth. Do not think of the people you are competing against or the person who is second. You have to convince your entire being that the whole Olympic stadium is for you. The members of the audience are eagerly supporting you and helping you in every possible way with their inner will and determination.

You have to feel that there is not a single human being who is against you, because you are not representing any particular country or race, but the entire earth.

So, while running, feel that the whole earth in a thunderous voice is repeating your name: "Carl Lewis, Carl Lewis, Carl Lewis." Then, when you are about to approach the board in the long jump, feel that the whole earth—all of humanity—is standing up. You do not have to see whether you have covered 9, 10 or 11 metres. Only feel that millions of human beings are standing up to honour you because you have broken Beamon's record and brought supreme glory to earth. This is what I advise you to do when you do the long jump.

As for your training, again I wish to tell you that every second of your life is of paramount importance now when the Olympics are fast approaching. So do what inspires you most inwardly, and do not surrender to the foul criticism of the outer world. The entire world knows what 100 metres is. So please pay all attention to the 100; the 50 and 60-metre events are of no importance.

The world cares for speed, so we have to prove that we are absolutely the fastest. How I wish all human beings would run faster than the fastest, with unimaginable speed, towards Eternity's ever-transcending Goal. Once we reach the highest transcendental Height with our fastest speed and consciously begin serving our Supreme Pilot at every moment, at that time we can and we shall create an absolutely new creation. At that time there will be only one reality, one song: the song of self-transcendence. There will be no boxing ring where might is right. There will be no destruction. In order to prove our supremacy, we will only have to transcend ourselves the way the Absolute Supreme is transcending Himself. The supreme secret or goal will be to transcend our own capacities. We will not try to defeat others. We will try only to constantly transcend ourselves. In this way we will get supreme satisfaction and offer supreme satisfaction to the inner world and to the outer world.

This is what our Beloved Absolute Supreme expects from His Creation, and He will be fully satisfied only when that type of reality manifests itself on earth. It may take thousands or millions of years, but He will not be fully satisfied until He has created that type of Creation. Let us pray and meditate to become consciously part and parcel of His new Creation. Let us try to become one, inseparably one, with His Will and, when the God-Hour arrives, to become the choice instruments in His tomorrow's Creation.

Advice at the 1988 Olympics

Sri Chinmoy went to Seoul, Korea to watch Carl Lewis compete in the 1988 Olympics, held from 17 September to 2 October. He met with the Olympic champion there on 25 September.

Sri Chinmoy: Now please tell me, why did you—a world champion—have to glance to the right side after 75 metres? Even a beginner, a novice, would first and foremost be advised not to do that. It is such a deplorable mistake! I was so sad when I saw you looking at Ben Johnson. Originally your goal was in front of you, but then you changed your goal. He became your goal instead of the tape.

You have such determination, such will-power, that you easily could have fought him right up to the end. But instead, you did not maintain your adamantine will, and after 75 metres you surrendered. How did it happen?

Carl Lewis: I have no explanation. When I saw he was so far out, I was shocked for the first time. You are right!

Sri Chinmoy: I am telling you, until the very last moment nothing is decided. In boxing there are 12 rounds. Even if someone is leading in points after the 11th round, still you can knock him out in the 12th round. Then he is gone! So if you knock him out, those points are not counted. Similarly, no matter how far you are behind someone else, all that matters is who touches the tape first. The goal is not won until then. Let us say he is winning the first few rounds. But those rounds do not mean anything. If you are determined that in the last round you are going to destroy him, then why do you have to worry about the first few rounds?

Carl Lewis: You really make it sink in!

Sri Chinmoy: I tell you these things to convince your mind. How many times Joe Lewis fell down, then stood up and defeated his opponent by a knockout. So this is the kind of attitude that you have to have, no matter how many metres ahead of you your opponent is. As soon as you look at him, you are entering into his consciousness, and your own consciousness you are losing. You are surprised and shocked that he is ahead of you. But when you are shocked you are invoking a kind of force inside yourself that enters into him and helps him. But if you only think of your goal, then you are entering into God's Consciousness, and God is helping you.

It is like this. When you think of your opponent—even if you are thinking of how you will defeat him—a little bit of your determination goes into him and adds to his capacity. But if you think only of your goal, then God comes to increase your determination.

Then there is something that you have to do only for me. To please me you have to do this! Please practise running 20 metres, and try to increase the length of your stride. You may not be able to do away with one full stride, but even if you can cut back by seven inches or a foot it will be very helpful. Your problem is with the first 20 metres. Even the quite inferior runners are keeping up with you during the first 20 metres, and there are even two or three runners ahead of you. I am watching you and taking pictures.

These runners are nowhere. After 40 metres your speed increases and you leave them in the dust. At the end of the 100 metres, they are 10 metres behind you. It is like seeing a little mouse ahead of a deer. The deer took a slow start, let us say, and the mouse is ahead. We know the deer is definitely going to win.

But in the beginning if you had the speed of that little mouse, you would do better. The speed you already have is tremendous, absolutely tremendous, but if you could add just a little bit to it, I would be so happy.

I am the worst possible runner, but I am telling you this on the strength of my oneness with your heart. I am worse than the worst, but I am advising the absolute best on the strength of my oneness, so that you can be better than the best. You are the best, but I am telling you to be better than the best in the first 20 metres. So many times I am seeing on the tape that your first 20 metres can be better.

Carl Lewis: I just have to work on it.

Sri Chinmoy: After 40 metres we do not worry. Then all the other runners fall away. But if you can cover the first 20 metres at their speed, then you will do even better. In no way are you going to get tired at the end if you have a most powerful start. It is absurd to say that you will not be able to maintain your speed.

We have one picture where the runner on your left has already gone while your foot is still in the air. At the end that poor fellow is nowhere, but in the beginning he is ahead of you. So if you had his speed at the beginning, you would be able to do much better.

Carl Lewis: Yes, I have a point where I say, "Now keep going, keep the pressure on!"

Sri Chinmoy: Mentally you are telling yourself to keep up the same speed. But you have to feel that you are like a machine. In the beginning when you switch on the machine, it starts running. But when you come to the second stage, you press another switch, and then it goes much faster—with volcanic speed. If you use the fastest speed at the start, you will only fall down. But after 50 metres, you have to convince your mind that there is another dynamo inside you which goes much faster than your starting speed. You have to feel that you have another tiny motor in you, which you will switch on after 50 metres, and that this motor is 10 or 20 times faster than the first motor. If you can convince your mind of this, if after 50 metres you can feel that you have turned on the second switch, then your mind will make you much faster. These things are not theoretical. In the beginning they may sound theoretical, but then they become practical, and you will go much faster.

Carl Lewis: I am convinced that I can run faster, too. Every year it has been better.

Sri Chinmoy: Our philosophy is to always make progress. But do not be disheartened by what has happened. Only feel that now Ben Johnson has got it and next it will be coming to you. I will be so happy if you can win in the next Olympics. The mind says, "O God, four years is so long to wait!" But you have to think of these four years as four months. If you can convince your mind that it is only four months, you are not fooling yourself; only you are touching another dimension and using another vision.

If you think of four years, all your determination goes away. You say, "Oh, I have plenty of time. Now let me enjoy a little rest." But if you think of the next Olympics as only four months away, then you will maintain your topmost determination. And the determination that you maintain will definitely increase your speed, and this increased speed will be your possession.

I really do not want you to wait another four years; I want this record to be broken in a year. I am seeing in the inner world that you have already done it. Outwardly you still have to do it, but inwardly you have already done it. So try to feel that in one year's time you will break it. Do not even think of one year. Think of one or two months. There will be lots of meets in which you can do it. So you have to be ready. After the Olympics, while the other runners are taking a little vacation, I want you to reach another plateau, another height. While the rest of the world is sleeping, that is the time for you to be fully awake. It is like trying to accumulate wealth. When you get better speed, it is like inner wealth that you have accumulated.

I really feel that after this Olympics you should not relax. After making a new world record you can relax. But right now do not accept defeat unless it is God's Will. In your case I know it is not God's Will. I am always ready to surrender to God's Will. If I know that I have done everything that I could do, if I have prayed and meditated and done everything that I am supposed to do, then I am ready to offer the results of my actions at God's Feet.

But in your case immediately the answer comes that you have not done everything. If you had done everything that you were supposed to do in your inner life and outer life, then you would not have looked at Ben Johnson after 75 metres. Unfortunately, what has happened has happened, although it is not God's Will. But now that it has happened, you have to feel that the past is dust. You have to believe in yourself today!

I am all for you. You have no idea how much I am for you. You are going to be 27 in July. I was born on the 27th—in August. You will be 31 in the next Olympics. I was born in '31. In my heart these things are all very important; these are very special, sacred, occult numbers. When you were running the 100 metres, I was holding an American flag. After you lost, a Canadian told me to put it down. I said, "Not for long, not for long." He looked at me and saw that I was very serious.

So please try these things that I am suggesting. You will also have our prayer and meditation, and your father's help from Heaven. Right now you have $100, let us say. Let us take the capacity that God has already given you as $100. We are trying to give you another dollar, so it becomes $101. If he gives you a dollar and she gives you a dollar, then it becomes $102, whereas your competitor only has his original $100. So these last two dollars that you are getting will help you go ahead of him.

I am so proud of you and grateful to you that you offered your gold medal to please your father's soul. [*Carl Lewis had placed the gold medal which he had won for the 100-metre event in the Los Angeles Olympics into his father's coffin.*] Right now your father is in another room. Previously he was in this room, and you were able to see and touch him. Now he is in another room, where you can only feel him. If you could open your third eye, which is the eye of vision, you could also see him.

You have boundless love and affection for your father, and he has boundless love and affection for you. Your feeling of love has entered into him in the soul's world, and his feeling of love has entered into you in the physical world. So he is offering considerable help to you. Also, God's Compassion, our good will, everything is for you. So you are getting great inner wealth.

Tomorrow is a big day for you. I will be there around nine o'clock. For tomorrow, no advice—only our prayers, good will and determination.

Your soul is your friend; your country is your friend. When it is a matter of sacrifice, you have to feel that America, your country, comes first. I really want America to be proud of you every second. In the case of Martin Luther King, for example, there is no white, no black; there is only appreciation, admiration and adoration, for he has conquered the hearts of all.

Similarly, when Carl Lewis comes into the picture, I want the people throughout the length and breadth of America to claim you as their very own. Your heart's sympathy, closeness and oneness will conquer the heart of the entire America. Look at your feeling of oneness! Ben Johnson is your greatest rival, but right after he defeated you, you went over and congratulated him.

My dearest Sudhahota,* we are not only all for you but only, only for you. That is what love has to be like. If I love someone only, then my concentration-power is not dispersed; it goes all to you and nobody can come in between.

---

*Sri Chinmoy offered Carl Lewis the spiritual name 'Sudhahota' (which means 'unparalleled sacrificer of Immortality's Nectar-Delight' in Bengali) when they first met in 1983.

Sri Chinmoy presenting the "Lifting Up the World with a Oneness-Heart" award to Paul Tergat several days before the Kenyan runner won the 2005 New York City Marathon.

7
ADVICE TO PAUL TERGAT

There is no such thing as impossibility
if our adamantine will comes from within.

Sri Chinmoy met with Kenyan marathon champion Paul Tergat several days before he won the 2005 New York City Marathon. Sri Chinmoy shared with Paul Tergat his prediction that soon someone would run the marathon in under two hours, and his hope that Tergat would be the first. He then offered him the following advice.

Just run and run, and while you are running the last mile, just think that a tiger is chasing you, so that you are running for your life. Think that a tiger is coming or think of something else that will inspire you.

After 25 miles, when you still have to cover one more mile, then you will feel that you are not running. Somebody else is running—that is God. Again, God may inspire you in and through some of His earthly Creations. It can be a field, it can be a forest or it can be a lake—anything that gives you utmost joy so that your tiredness and fatigue will be transformed into your firmness.

When you are at 25 miles, one mile more to go, please try to feel that you have completed the marathon. The indomitable joy that you will get from within will carry you through the last mile. The first 25 miles run. Then try to feel that somebody else, God, is going to run this mile in and through you.

At the very start, you have dedicated the marathon to God, to the Will of God, and the results you will place at the Feet of God. That you have to do, either cheerfully or sorrowfully. But then, once you have covered 25 miles, feel that the last mile God is running. God has been running inwardly in and through you, but this time try to feel God is running outwardly as well. The last mile God is running.

You are watching and admiring Someone who is running so fast, so fast. That Person is God, not you. You are only observing Him, seeing Him, appreciating Him, admiring Him and adoring Him, saying, "O my God, how fast He is running!" You will have to forget that you are running. At that moment feel you are not running. Paul Tergat is not running. Somebody else in the Name of God is running in and through you.

In that way, your four minutes will disappear [i.e. your marathon time will go from 2:04 to 2:00], and you will be able to run under 2 hours. There is nothing impossible if you try. The 'impossibility' word is found only in the dictionary, but not in the heart, not in the fulfilment of our dreams. The dictionary says 'impossible.' It is the mind. From the brain the word came into existence.

When we enter into the heart, the story completely changes. Please forgive me, I am not boasting here. I am getting older. Now I have seen 74 summers and winters. When I was on the wrong side of 50 I started weightlifting. Now I am lifting weights that I could not lift in those days, 10 or 15 years ago. I am lifting much heavier weights. In some cases I am holding world records at the age of 74. This is unbelievable, and at the same time, undeniable.

There is no such thing as impossibility. If our adamantine will comes from within that we are going to do something, nobody can prevent it. Do not use the mind. A child does not use the mind. He just runs and runs and runs. He never becomes tired. Then when we grow up, after five minutes, the mind makes us feel that we have worked very, very hard. We now deserve a rest.

If you can feel you are that little child at the age of five or six or seven years old, that unlimited energy again will be bestowed upon you, specially during the last mile. Please at that time surrender to God's Will, and you be the observer. You observe who is running so fast, and you admire that person.

Everybody has to feel that God is performing His Will in and through each individual in a unique way. Yours is 'run, run, run, and be the champion of champions, break the world record, under 2 hours.' Today's dream is tomorrow's reality. Now you are dreaming of something, and tomorrow it will turn into reality.

Thousands of years ago our forefathers dreamt of a world that will have continuous progress, progress, progress. Success and progress will go together. Here in the outer life it is success. In the inner life it is progress. Again, when we make progress, we are really happy. Success does not last. Progress is something everlasting, whereas success is a fleeting experience, just for today. But the inner progress that we make, that is only for us to enjoy, and nobody else.

Success you have already. You are the champion of champions. How many times you have won long distance races and marathons. But progress is something else. Now if you break the world record, that is your progress. From 2:04, you are going to run under two [hours]. That progress lasts forever, as long as you are on earth. But if we take it as success, then we are miserable. Tomorrow somebody will break our record.

Bill Rodgers, the marathon champion 20 years ago, said, "My records will go." He knew that his records were not going to last. Here is the proof. His time was, I think, 2:09. His record you have smashed. But now if you can take this as your progress, inner and outer progress, then everything is possible, possible.

This is my feeling about you, my inner feeling. I am echoing and re-echoing your message: impossibility does not exist. Please, please, today's dream you transform into reality.

8
QUESTIONS FROM CHAMPION RUNNERS

Your world-surprising potential is ahead of you and beckoning you.

Most of these questions from world-class runners were answered by Sri Chinmoy in 1982 and 1983 and published on a monthly basis in a syndicated column entitled "Run and Become." Biographical information on the runners is provided in the Appendix.

Craig Virgin: How can I cope with the pressure of winning or, on the other hand, the disappointment of losing in a sports competition?

You can cope with the pressure of winning if, a few days before the race or even just before the start, you can imagine the pleasure of rejoicing in your victory. Imagination is not wishful thinking; it is not a baseless reality. Imagination is reality itself in another world. We bring it down to this world the way we bring down fruits from a tree.

To cope with the disappointment of losing, you have to ask yourself whether the mind is disappointed or the heart is disappointed. You will realise that it is your mind that is disappointed and not your heart. The mind creates division; the mind is division itself, and division is another name for pain, devastating pain. The heart, on the other hand, creates oneness; in fact, the heart is oneness itself, and oneness is another name for joy, spontaneous joy. When you live in your heart, even if your worst rival wins the race, you will not feel miserable. To your wide surprise, you will find that his joy quite unconsciously and unexpectedly will enter into you and widen your heart. Then you will feel almost the same joy that the winner feels.

It was your heart that was speaking in and through this illumining utterance of yours: "Running is the people's sport. When was the last time the average person played ball with Reggie Jackson? Yet millions of people run in the same races and rub elbows with the top runners. In what other sport can the average player run the same course and go through the same trials as the top stars?"

You are sharp, very sharp; bright, very bright; quick, very quick. And something quite rare in the running world—you have intuition. Your intuitive faculties remarkably add to your success in racing. To our great joy and satisfaction, your body, vital, mind and heart speedily and breathlessly follow your intuitive flashes.

John Dimick: What should a good runner do when he finds that the pressures of his family, community and job mean he cannot train at high mileage or undertake frequent racing?

In order to become such an excellent runner, you have already made a great many sacrifices in terms of expending time and energy and giving up the comfortable, pleasure-loving world. Now, if you go one step ahead and train at high mileage or undertake frequent racing, you may lose your job, but you will not lose your family or community, to be sure. As a result of your tremendous successes, the temporary pressures you have to undergo from the members of your family will all be transformed into innocent and enriching treasures. And there is every possibility that you will get a better job at a higher salary because of your greater successes.

You are a superb runner. For you the hour has struck. Those who are even unconsciously standing in your way will one day cheerfully and unreservedly support you. Please feel that you have already started a race. Now your only aim is to reach the goal, no matter how many obstacles you have to surmount on the way. Your victory will ultimately be the victory of your dear ones and also the victory of the entire world running community.

It is my earnest request to you that you practise as many miles as you want to and run as many races as you want to. When the pressures you now face are transformed into treasures, not only your dear ones but also all and sundry will deeply value and gratefully enjoy them.

Eamonn Coghlan: Given an Olympic final, ten competitors are lined up in the race, and all are 100 per cent physically fit and prepared, what does it take for one runner to win over the others?

It is not just a matter of luck as to who wins. There are two ways to become a winner: one way is to concentrate on each runner and, like a magnet, draw into oneself the will-power that each one has. In that way, you almost empty the other runners of their will-power or life-energy. This is called sheer determination-power. The determination-lion devours the weaker animals.

The other way is to identify oneself with the Source of the fastest speed and endurance. Here one consciously becomes one with the higher realities that are invisible, yet infinitely faster and stronger than the outer realities or, let us say, the outer capacities. If a runner is a conscious truth-seeker and God-lover, then he will adopt the inner way and not the outer way. The outer way is the way of the lion: roaring and devouring the rivals.

Don Kardong: Why do you think runners are often able to achieve a meditative state while running?

Concentration, meditation and contemplation are three members of the same family. When a runner focusses all his attention on a particular race, he is in a position to free his mind from uncomely distractions. Here one-pointed concentration is the pathfinder for a deeper, meditative consciousness.

Don Kardong: What role should competition play in one's running?

If the runner is a seeker, then he has a special role. His role is to compete with himself and try to increase his own capacity. But he will increase his capacity only by virtue of the infinite Grace of God, if so is the Will of God. So the seeker-runner will try to consciously surrender to the Will of God during his running career.

Dick Beardsley: Recently I ran a 2:08:53 marathon with primarily a road-racing background. Would it improve my chances of making the 1984 Olympic marathon team if I partake in training and racing the 10,000 metres on the track? If I get the speed down in 10,000 metres, will I run a faster marathon?

Definitely you will improve your marathon time if you run 10,000 metres on the track. Running is a physical subject, a mental subject, a philosophical subject and a subject of the Beyond. In the physical aspect, nobody will be able to tell you more than you already know. In the mental aspect, if you become used to running shorter distances, it can really help you.

When you are running a marathon, mentally try to feel that you are running only thirteen miles rather than twenty-six miles. If you can convince the mind of this fact, and if the mind can convince the body that it is running only thirteen miles and not twenty-six miles, then it will be a great advantage for you. This is not a mental hallucination. A new discovery has dawned in the mind and the mind is passing it along to the body. Both the mind and the body will have to act together in order to reach the ultimate goal.

In the philosophical aspect, you have to feel that your problems are as insignificant as ants and pay no attention to them. You have had problems with cows, dogs, puddles and road hazards of all kinds. You should take these problems philosophically. Although these things are extremely unfortunate and discouraging for a great runner like you, you have to feel that they are almost part and parcel of a runner's life. If you can see them in this way, then when discouragement and temporary lack of enthusiasm attack you, you can easily, successfully and fruitfully overcome these obstacles on the way to your sublime goal.

Finally, if you can think that through your running you are doing something that has a direct connection with the ever-transcending Beyond, which is far beyond the domain of the earth-bound physical mind, then you will get tremendous inspiration. This inspiration embodies added strength, added joy and an added sense of satisfaction.

In your case, it seems to me that mentally you are not confident of your fastest speed. Either because of your own personal experience or because of ideas that others have thrust upon you, you feel that you do not possess extraordinary speed, specially towards the end of a race when speed is badly required.

To get rid of this absurd notion for good, twice a week try to run between thirty and fifty metres as fast as possible, at intervals of a minute or even longer, for twenty-five or thirty consecutive times. Your mind will all of a sudden be fully awakened to a new discovery of your own speed, which has all along been unnoticed, if not ignored. This mental discovery will help you considerably.

Kindly try this new method and the other suggestions that I have offered. Although you are a great runner, you still have not yet reached your highest potential. Your world-surprising potential is ahead of you and beckoning you.

Gary Fanelli: Sometimes when I am racing, I ask myself, "What am I doing here, beating my brains and body out?" I've had some injuries, but I continue racing. What is the best attitude towards this?

Dear Gary, you are an excellent runner. When you run fast, please try to feel that your speed itself is a great success. Try to feel that through your success in running, humanity is taking one step forward in its march towards its ever-transcending goal.

You are an American. Americans take life as a challenge from the cradle to the grave. When you run, you are challenging yourself and nobody else. When you work very hard in your running and get severe injuries, you should try to have a divine attitude. Try to feel that the constant increase in your capacity to endure pain is of paramount importance. When you increase your capacities, automatically you establish a glowing hope and a soaring promise for your fellow runners all over the world.

Questions from Champion Runners

Cahit Yeter: After averaging nearly 7,000 miles over the past three years, I believe I have satisfied my thirst for very long, long runs. Meanwhile, I am still entering many long races. Most of the time, winning itself does not come into my mind, but sometimes I think of running beyond the records most other men have run. I'd like to know, since winning is everything in America and I am part of it, why I have lost my desire to win.

My dear brother-friend, you are an ultramarathoner par excellence. You have covered thousands and thousands of miles in the past few years. You have also given us, your dear friends, boundless joy. It is true that winning is everything in America. Again, you have to know that there are two kinds of races: the outer race and the inner race. There are also two kinds of desire: the outer desire and the inner desire, which we call aspiration. The outer desire says, "Run, reach, then smile." The inner desire says, "Smile and run, run and smile. The goal is nowhere else save and except in smiling and running, and running and smiling."

You have won an amazing number of races on the strength of your outer desire. Now aspiration, the inner desire, has come to the fore. It wants to play its role most significantly in you, just as the outer desire has played its role over the years. Until now you have exercised your outer desire to conquer the world and show what you possess in order to draw the world's attention and admiration. You are now trying to exercise your inner desire to show the world what you have to offer for the world's improvement, which is an intrinsic part of your own improvement. Previously you wanted victory for your own satisfaction, and that victory you achieved by defeating others. Now you want the victory that comes from the satisfaction of establishing oneness, genuine oneness, with others.

A radiant example of your oneness we saw recently when you ran in our Sri Chinmoy Marathon held in New York. Out of your loving, sympathetic oneness-heart you asked that your prize be given to the runner who came in last. Such is your feeling for your fellow runners! For you, they are like members of your own family. As the older one who is more experienced, you encourage the younger ones to come forward by spreading your joy and satisfaction all around. Fortunately or unfortunately, one of the members of our team stood last, and she was deeply moved to receive your trophy.

Mary Decker Slaney: It is known that some female athletes, because of drugs, have a chemical advantage over their competitors. How can a natural athlete, such as myself, justify the use of world rankings, knowing that other athletes using drugs are consistently ranked higher than so-called natural athletes?

Sometimes it is good and necessary to know what others are doing. If one is a runner, this can encourage one's competitive spirit. Again, sometimes it is a great hindrance when we know what others are doing. It puzzles us and, at the same time, we have no inclination to adopt their methods. In cases like this it is always good to depend on one's own natural ability.

Nature embodies the cosmic energy. This cosmic energy is infinitely stronger than any man-made chemicals. This energy comes from the ultimate Source and it leads us to the ultimate Source while fulfilling and satisfying us along the way. Chemicals and other artificial things will ultimately fail, for they are unnatural. Anything that is unnatural is like a balloon. For a while it will dazzle us and puzzle our human mind, but eventually it will burst.

One of my poems speaks about naturalness. It says:

> **Live in naturalness**
> **If you want to grow**
> **Into the fulness**
> **Of God's Vision-Reality.**

Stay with your natural ability. Already you are a radiant example of nature's unquestionable supremacy over the so-called chemical miracles. You have been chosen as the US Athlete of the Year. You can definitely bring high, higher and highest glories in the running world not only to your beloved country, America, but to all humanity.

Greg Meyer: Why do I get more satisfaction from training than from racing?

You get more satisfaction from your training than from your racing because when you train, you have more oneness with your inner life, which embodies infinite satisfaction. When you race, you are competing with others because you want to defeat them. The challenging spirit that comes in competition quite often suffers from anxiety, worry, doubt, hesitation and despair. When you are just practising, however, you are performing before the most intimate members of your family—your body, vital, mind, heart, and soul. In fact, these intimate members of your own being are practising and performing with you, in you and for you. It is totally a family entertainment.

While practising, you are consciously working to transcend your capacities. At that time, you are listening to the message of the ever-transcending Beyond, and the message itself is complete satisfaction. But when you compete against others, you are more concerned with victory than with self-transcendence. Naturally, at that time hesitation, anxiety and doubt have free access to your heart and mind and you do not and cannot have satisfaction.

But when you practise, you and your aspiration, you and your dedication, you and your eagerness to increase your capacities work together for your improvement and perfection. And from improvement and perfection, you are bound to get abiding satisfaction.

Because of the feeling of separativity in the mind, we may get fleeting satisfaction when we defeat others. But perhaps quite a few times during our practice we had more illumining and more fulfilling satisfaction, for practice carries the message of oneness and self-transcendence, whereas competition carries the message of division and supremacy.

Rod Dixon: Am I being reasonable to expect my family to understand my physical urge to pursue my running life? I want to please my family, yet I also want to please my running career.

You are a great runner. Already you have achieved astonishing glories in your running career. In order to achieve such sublime heights in the running world, you have made tremendous sacrifices, and the members of your family also have made tremendous sacrifices. This kind of mutual sacrifice is in no way an indication of your negligence towards your family. In the course of thinking of the ultimate or meditating on the ultimate, along the way you make apparent sacrifices. You have to know that eventually these sacrifices themselves become a source of illumining satisfaction or they will pale into insignificance when you are repeatedly crowned with Himalayan success.

With their human hearts, the members of your immediate family want to possess you and have you all the time around them. Your affection and love for them and their affection and love for you mean everything to them. Perhaps your running laurels are secondary to them. But again, these same members of your family each has a divine heart. Unlike the human heart, which wants to possess and be possessed, the divine heart wants only to give of itself, widen itself, receive the vast world and be received by the vast world. These are the messages that the divine heart receives from the higher worlds and offers to the outer world at large.

Those who live in the divine heart are meant for the whole world. The messages that this heart gives them they do not keep secretly and sacredly inside their immediate family. No, they offer these messages to all of humanity. So if any want to possess you or want to claim you as their own, very own, they should try to live in the divine heart, just as you are doing.

If you and also the members of your immediate family can all live in the divine heart, then your commitment to your dear ones and their full understanding of what you were, what you are and what you are going to become will eventually and unmistakably bring boundless joy and boundless satisfaction to you and also to them.

You come from New Zealand and you now live in America. Like the members of your family, New Zealand may think that it has lost you. But if we look at the truth from a new angle, then we see that, like the members of your family, your country does not actually lose you when you go abroad to run. The way the members of your family have offered you to the world at large, to be claimed by the entire world, New Zealand also has offered you to the world. Yet it can and does still claim your astounding triumphs as its own, very own.

Not only are you bringing tremendous glory to your beloved country, New Zealand, but you are also bringing glory to America and to the entire world. Nobody loses anything. All of us only gain—not only for our personal selves or for the members of our immediate families, but also for the community of nations, for the entire world.

When we use our wisdom-light, we illumine our ignorance-night and add abiding satisfaction to our own small worlds and also to the vast world that is around us.

Mike Spino: If higher states of consciousness are possible when running, will this always result in superlative performances? Can there be a poor performance and a gain in the life quest? If so, how can this be recognised?

It is not guaranteed that if one is in a high state of consciousness, one will perform extremely well. Sixteen thousand runners ran in this year's New York Marathon. I do not want to brag, but I do not think that ten or eleven thousand of them had a higher consciousness than the poor runner in me; but they still defeated me. So capacity is of paramount importance. But along with capacity, if one can invoke a higher consciousness, then one is likely to do very well. Again, we have to know that an increase in capacity comes quite often not only from regular training but also from the descent of Grace, which is part and parcel of a higher consciousness.

Mike Spino: In our last meeting I was fortunate to have you observe a film of the late Percy Cerutty demonstrating his canter and gallop techniques. You made insightful commentary on the nature of his spirit as it related to this late phase of his life. Could you elaborate further?

First of all, I wish to tell you that your article on the great Australian coach Percy Cerutty is most remarkable. I had read Cerutty's famous book and I learned much about running. But I did not know much about the man. Your article made it clearer to me how he wanted people to run and also told me a lot about Cerutty, the real man.

When I observed your simple but moving and soulful film of Cerutty in the evening of his life, I saw an unusually indomitable spirit encaged in a lean earthly frame. To me, it seems that the power aspect of Cerutty came more to the fore than his compassion and love aspect. Some took him to be an eccentric while others admired him for his staunch belief in people's inner and hidden capacities. To me, he was neither a lunatic nor a fanatic. I found him to be uniquely dynamic. But this dynamism of his was sadly misunderstood by many critics.

Mike Spino: America is seeking a form of an Olympic training centre, yet the American lifestyle negates the use of any mental training that is larger than biofeedback or personality inventory. As a university coach seeking a mental training technique with objective timings, how does one balance the objectives of a programme? Is it a 'given' that as we seek dual purposes of spirituality and performance, we will remain an iconoclast, understood by only a small circle and questioning our own methods?

It is quite likely that you will be understood by only a small circle because most runners are either unaware of the inner realities or are apt to feel that the inner realities cannot be manifested in the outer world. The inner realities are for the inner world; the outer realities are for the outer world: this is what they think. But no, the inner realities, meaning the inner capacities, must be executed on the outer plane. The seed must germinate; it has to grow into a plant and then into a huge banyan tree.

Mike Spino: I have experimented with moving visualisations in an attempt to transfer 'sitting awareness' to running consciousness. What suggestions can you make for this transfer, and is sitting a necessary prerequisite for the development of elated running consciousness?

Always think that you are standing in front of the sea. The surface of the sea is very dynamic; it is all waves and surges. But the bottom of the sea is all calmness and peace. You can identify yourself with the surface of the sea and also with its depths. Similarly, you can identify with both the outer world and the inner world. While looking at the outer life, you see dynamism and speed. But even while you are looking at the outer life you can dive into the inner life, where it is all peace and inner poise. If you dive within and become inseparably one with inner peace, then easily you can bring inner peace to the fore so that it inundates your outer life.

'Sitting awareness' is stillness, calmness, quietness, while the running consciousness is all dynamism. Again, the runner's outer speed has a special kind of poise or stillness at its very heart. A plane travels very fast, yet inside the plane we feel no movement at all. It is all tranquillity, all peace, and this inner tranquillity we can bring to our outer life. The outer life, the outer movement, can be successful only when it comes from inner poise. If there is no poise, then there can be no successful outer movement. Poise is an unseen power, and this unseen power is always ready to come to the aid of the outer runner.

Following are excerpts from a conversation between Sri Chinmoy and Robert Zmelik, Czech Olympic gold medallist in the decathlon, that took place in New York on 19 June 1996.

If you practise your 100 metres more, it will definitely, definitely help you in your long jump and in other items as well. But if you give more importance than is due to 1500 metres, then it will ruin your long jump and high jump. You are an excellent sprinter. One hundred metres, shot-put, long jump and high jump go together because of the speed and the spring that are needed. The first thing that 1500 metres does is take away the spring. No matter how slowly you run, 1500 metres is so bad for sprinters. Up to 400 metres you can practise, but 800 or 1500 metres is bad for sprinters. You can get stamina, but stamina is not speed. If you practise 800 metres, it may help you get stamina for 400 metres, but if you practise 800 metres more, definitely you will lose some spring for your 100 metres.

You will not get endurance for the decathlon from running long distance. You have to get endurance by practising the individual events. Suppose you are doing shot-put or discus. You do not have to do your best performance; you do not have to use your maximum capacity. You can increase your endurance not by running 1500 metres, but by practising the events that you are already very good in. For example, you can do two or three hurdles instead of ten hurdles to get stamina. Then in pole-vault, you can jump, but not at your maximum height. For stamina, you can do the pole-vault at a very low height. If you want to get endurance and stamina, you can practise the items that will not take away your spring. If you run 1500 metres, it will ruin your spring, and then it will affect your high jump and your long jump.

The 1500 is nothing—less than four rounds on the track—but if you practise it many times, then your spring disappears. So kindly be very careful with your 100 metres, long jump, shot-put and high jump. Definitely I want you to do well in 1500 metres, but not by running it more times. You can increase your stamina in some other way. If you want to, you can even try sprinting 30 or 40 metres many times. You know your speed for 100 metres, so you can do it a few times more to get stamina.

So many items in the decathlon depend on speed. The shot-put definitely requires speed. It comes from the elbow or from the shoulder or somewhere else, but speed is absolutely necessary. Even very strong people cannot throw the shot well if they have no speed, and that speed you have.

How much time do you spend in taking exercises, such as weightlifting? How many days per week do you lift weights?

Robert Zmelik: I was lifting four times weekly, but now I do it two times a week. Now I am in a special programme using a medicine ball, with exercises for the abdominals and the torso. These are very important for turning and for force. Your record of 7,000 crunch sit-ups is unbelievable! I do 500, and then my abdomen hurts!

In your case, you have to compete in ten events. You do not need to do something like 7,000 sit-ups. My only suggestion to you is that this coming month, before the Olympics, you should not adopt anything new that you have not done before. If you want to increase, increase; if you want to decrease, decrease. But do not be greedy to try something new. Whatever you are doing, you can do the same thing a few times more or a few times less. But you are taking a great risk if you try to practise anything new. Many athletes make that mistake. It is our eagerness or greed: "If I do this, perhaps I will do better." At that time problems will arise because you have a very, very high standard. At this standard when you want to adopt something new, you take a risk. But the things that you have been doing are safe. If you want to do more repetitions or fewer repetitions, you can. Only do the things that you have been familiar with for at least six months. Anything new at this point, when it is only a matter of a month, may create problems because you are not accustomed to it.

You may feel, "Oh, this may help me." It may help you, true, but again it may create some problem for you. The last month before the competition, everything you must do with utmost confidence. You will throw, run and jump with utmost confidence. If you adopt something new, at that time you may not have confidence. When you do not have confidence, that is the time when you may get injuries. Confidence removes all fear and doubt. If we do something new, we may get freshness in our mind, but again the same mind can give us doubt. If we do something for the first time, we can have tremendous happiness because it is a new adventure. Again, when we want to enjoy a new adventure, we may be attacked by self-doubt. This is not the time for you to have any kind of self-doubt in anything you do. Everything you have to do with utmost confidence—you have done it, you have done it, you have done it. But if it is something new, you may not be able to say that, because you do not have the preparation from before.

So everything that you practise—shot-put, discus, javelin, jumping or running—do with utmost confidence because you have been doing it for so many years. But if you feel that by taking a particular exercise or by doing something else, you will increase your capacity, you will be entering into new territory, an unknown field. That unknown field can give you beautiful flowers or it can give you something else.

Suprabha Beckjord: For an ultramarathon that goes on for many days, do I need to have patience or should I just try to have dynamism?

Every morning, when you are starting to run, you have to feel that this is the only day that you are running. Then, when tomorrow comes, again think that this is the only day. Otherwise, you may lose patience when you have to run more than a month. To try to always maintain dynamism is out of the question. Every day when you start, if you can convince yourself that it is only for one day, then you will think, "Oh, I can easily do it. Only last year I ran 3100 miles. Today I cannot run 60 miles? Easily I can do it!" Since quite often the mind is fooling us, we have to use our wisdom to fool the mind.

Suprabha Beckjord: Is there some spiritual quality that I can invoke during the 3100-mile race this year to really please the Supreme? Outwardly I know the goal is to finish the race and to transcend my best time, but is there something I can do inwardly to please the Supreme?

What qualities do you need to bring forward from your inner life while you are running? The first one is enthusiasm. Who embodies enthusiasm? A little child. Who can be more enthusiastic than a child? Then, in addition to enthusiasm, you need eagerness. Again, who has more eagerness than a little child? If he plays with a toy, he is so eager, his whole world is the toy.

Every day when you run, you have to feel that it is the golden opportunity to appreciate the One who is inspiring you. Always you have to feel that the Supreme is inspiring you to run this longer than the longest distance. When you run, if you offer the prayer, "God, please make me a good runner. I want to make progress this time in my running," then this is a good prayer. At that time, God Himself will become a good runner inside you.

While running 3100 miles, you have to deal with fatigue. Many days you are tired, exhausted, dead. As long as you are in the mind, you will always have fatigue, tiredness, weariness and everything. But the moment you enter into the heart, there is no fatigue. What you will find is constant energy. If you are in the heart, there is a constant supply of energy and sweetness. We all have to develop sweetness. Sweetness is a reality which is constantly supplying us with newness and freshness.

Early in the morning when you get up, if you have a sweet feeling inside you, then everything is beautiful. If inside you there is sweetness, the whole world is beautiful. But if inside you there is bitterness, then no matter what you see, you will not get any joy. Even if you look at a beautiful flower, there will be no joy. But inner sweetness sees the world as most beautiful.

When you are running around, after an hour or two hours or a few days, you start thinking, "This is so bad. Every day I have to do sixty miles," this and that. But who counts the mileage? It is the mind. The mind is saying, "O my God, today I have to do sixty miles, and I have not yet done twenty miles!" Then you are finished! The mind, your worst enemy, is coming to torture you.

But the heart is not counting the mileage. The heart is only running, running, running. Then at the end of that session, the heart says, "Now let me see how many miles I have done." By that time, perhaps you have done forty miles already. The heart does not calculate. The mind calculates from one to two, two to three, three to four and so on. The mind tries to go to the destination by cutting, cutting, cutting. But the heart tries to see and feel the starting point and the end at the same time.

If you can feel that you are a five-year-old or six-year-old child, tiredness will not come into your mind. A child does not know what tiredness is. He knows only enthusiasm and eagerness. Never think of sixty miles or 3100 miles. Never take the distance in that way—never! Only run for the joy of it. When you run for the joy, even while you are running, sometimes you are thinking of something very divine and sweet. Then by the time you would have normally come to nineteen miles, you will have covered twenty-three miles. When the heart runs, you will have already run much more, and then you will say, "How could I have come so far?" The answer is because at that time you were in another world. The divinity of that other world was constantly helping you and supporting you.

When you run, never think that you are forty-three or forty-four years old. Only think that you are six or seven years old. If you are only six or seven years old, then why do you have to worry? When I lift heavy weights, at that time do I say, "O my God, I am sixty-nine, nearing seventy years old. How am I going to lift?" Then I would be finished! I will only go there and say, "O my God, it may drop on my head! I will die or have to live in the hospital the rest of my life." This is the kind of idea that the mind will supply me with.

But the heart does not see the weight in that way. The heart sees the weight as a big toy. When a child gets a toy, it may be so big that he cannot move it even, but he is so happy that such a big toy has now come into his possession. In my case, I take the weight as a toy. In your case also, when you think of the long distance, try to imagine that it is something to play with. Do not think of distance as something you will cover. Do not think that you will be tired, you will be exhausted or you will die. You have to take running as a game you like to play. Choose any game that you like, and feel that you are playing that game. Do not feel that you are running such a long distance, and that every day you are getting tired. No! With tiredness comes sadness, and then you become upset.

Each day when you go out to run, you should see newness, newness, newness. Always think of the heart-garden. When you walk or run in a garden, you do not become tired because of the beautiful flowers and fragrance. Everything is charming, everything is inspiring.

When your mind is operating very powerfully, you are not the boss. Your boss is self-doubt, self-criticism, fear, worry and anxiety. You are constantly thinking, "Will I be able to complete the race?" Those negative thoughts become your boss. But when you run inside your heart, at that time your boss is your love of God; your boss is your surrender to God's Will. If you can keep that feeling in your outer life while you are running, then there will be no problem.

Do not run with the mind. Even if today you fool the mind, tomorrow the mind will come back with redoubled trickeries to make your life miserable. You should say to the mind, "You stay with your trickeries. I want to play with my heart-toy, not with you. The heart-toy always brings me happiness and newness, newness and happiness."

When you run, if you can make yourself feel that inside your heart Somebody is running or your heart is running or you are running with your heart, then tiredness disappears, the power of distance disappears. Only the power of oneness, oneness, oneness with God's Will appears.

9
INTERVIEWS WITH JOURNALISTS

*Running and physical fitness help us
both in our inner life of aspiration
and in our outer life of activity.*

Following are excerpts from an interview with Nils Lodin of Spring-Time, a Swedish running magazine, which took place at the United Nations on 26 October 1982, two days after both Mr. Lodin and Sri Chinmoy had run the New York City Marathon.

How does running relate to your philosophy?

The body is like a temple and the soul or inner reality is like the shrine inside the body-temple. If the temple does not have a shrine, then we cannot appreciate the temple. Again, if we do not keep the temple in good condition, then how can we take proper care of the shrine? We have to keep the body fit, and for this, running is of considerable help. If we are physically fit, then we will be more inspired to get up early in the morning to meditate.

True, the inspiration to meditate comes from within, but if we are healthy, then it will be much easier for us to get up at five or six o'clock to pray and meditate. In this way the inner life is being helped by the outer life. Again, if we are inspired to get up early to meditate, then we will also be able to go out and run. Here we see that the outer life is being helped by the inner life.

Both outer running and inner running are important. A marathon is twenty-six miles. Let us say that twenty-six miles is our ultimate goal. When we first take up running, we cannot run that distance. But by practising every day, we develop more stamina, speed and perseverance. Gradually we transcend our limited capacity, and eventually we reach our goal. In the inner life our prayer and meditation is our inner running. If we pray and meditate every day, we increase our inner capacity.

The body's capacity and the soul's capacity, the body's speed and the soul's speed, go together. The outer running reminds us of something higher and deeper—the soul—which is running along Eternity's Road. Running and physical fitness help us both in our inner life of aspiration and in our outer life of activity.

Running has no value in itself?

Running helps us considerably. Running is continuous motion. Because of our running, we feel that there is a goal—not only an outer goal but also an inner goal. Running helps us by showing us that there is a goal. Again, running itself is a goal for those who want to keep the body in perfect condition.

Running offers us the message of transcendence. In our running, every day we are aiming at a new goal. It is like a child who studies in school. First he studies in kindergarten, then he goes to primary school, then to high school, college and university. After getting his university degree, still he is not satisfied. He wants to achieve more wisdom, more knowledge. Similarly, every day we are running towards a goal, but when we reach that goal, we want to go still farther. Either we want to improve our timing or increase our distance. There is no end. Running means continual transcendence, and that is also the message of our inner life.

When you are running a marathon, are you suffering?

It is a kind of experience that I am having.

It is a tough experience.

I get two kinds of experiences. On the physical, vital and mental planes, I get the experience which you call suffering. It is an unpleasant feeling. Again, there is also the inner experience. I feel that the outer experience is something that my Inner Pilot wants me to do, and I surrender the results to Him. I know it will take me more than four and a half hours. But if I can offer the results to Him, then I am getting a divine experience, the experience of surrender. One experience I am getting on the physical, vital and mental planes, and another experience I am getting on the psychic plane. Whatever I achieve, cheerfully I will give to Him; this is my inner experience.

The Inner Running and the Outer Running

I always say to my friends that you do not know anything about life until you have run a full marathon. It gives a dimension to life that I have never encountered before. The pain in those last six or eight miles is a pain that you cannot meet in other situations.

Right! We get a very unusual experience. We expect at every moment that the members of our inner family—the body, vital, mind and heart—will come to our rescue. I as an individual will think that since I have a body, a vital, a mind and a heart, naturally, now that I am in need of their help, these members of my family will come to my rescue. But after a few miles, they all revolt. They all say, "Give up! Get off the course!" We beg the body to carry us to the finish line, but the body is not listening. The vital also is not listening and the mind is constantly rejecting the idea. Determination we lose. So you are absolutely right. When one runs a marathon or any long distance, one knows what life is—a struggle from the beginning to the end. A marathon gives us a prime example of the struggle of human life.

The following is an interview conducted by Robert Swan, the editor of Simply Living *Magazine, on 14 September 1984 in Canberra, Australia.*

You have said that your philosophy is a merging of the inner and the outer. Most people would interpret meditation as being an inner process and I wonder if you could explain for us how you feel marathon running has a place in spiritual development.

The inner running and the outer running complement each other. For outer running, we need discipline. Without a life of discipline, we cannot succeed in any walk of life. So when we do outer running, it reminds us of the inner running. The inner running, we know, is the longest distance, eternal distance. We do not know when it started and we have no idea when we are going to end it. Whereas, if it is a marathon, we know that after covering 26 miles and 385 yards, we come to an end.

For outer running, we need a life of discipline, endurance and patience—so many things which are good! In the spiritual life also we need many things—we have to conquer our fear, doubt, jealousy, insecurity and so on. So we feel that one is helping the other.

Early in the morning, if I have freshness in my mind and if I have sound health, then I will be inspired to pray and meditate. If I do not have good health, then I am not going to get up and pray and meditate. So it is my good health that is helping me to become a good seeker.

Again, if I am a true seeker, then I will try to do something for mankind on the physical plane. If I love God the Creator, I must also love God the Creation, otherwise what kind of love is it? If I love God, who has created this world, I must also love the Creation itself. So while we run outwardly, it is the Creation that we see and when we pray and meditate, we are trying to have a conscious awareness of the Creator.

Does that mean that people who are not physically healthy cannot reach enlightenment?

Oh, no, most definitely they can. The only thing is that we do not have to be the strongest man, we do not have to be a boxer or wrestler, no. I am saying that early in the morning if I do not have stomach upset or headache or fever, if I am running or doing some other physical activity, then it helps me a lot. Otherwise, if I enter into the Himalayan caves and start praying and meditating and neglecting the body, then how many days can I go on, how many weeks, how many months?

There are some people who tend to neglect the body, the needs of the body. We are not saying that we have to become the world's greatest boxers or wrestlers, no. Only we should try to maintain a basic fitness. If I am physically fit, then I will be able to get up early in the morning. Then I can pray and meditate. If I am physically unfit, will I have the capacity to pray and meditate?

I have heard from some teachers in the Shankaracharya tradition that yoga asanas [postures] are good because they lower the metabolism of the body and help lay the foundation for meditation. But running, or Western sport, would seem to be in the other direction. You do not see it in this way?

No, no, no, because I have practised these things. It is only that hatha yoga is an Indian way of thinking and there was a time when whatever the Westerners did was very bad and whatever we Indians did was always good. For some time it was difficult for Indians to see anything good in the West. So the Indian theory was that our asanas are by far the best and the Western way of approaching the reality was wrong.

Now I wish to say that there should be a combination of the Indian spirit, which is calm, quiet and tranquil, and the Western spirit, which is dynamic. We have to take them as one. The Indians think that the West is all restlessness, which is not true. And again, the West thinks that India is all poverty-stricken and Indians are lethargic, which is also not true. Both sides exaggerate the facts.

When we think of the West, we have to think of the good quality of the West, which is dynamism. And when we think of the East, let us say India, we have to think of calmness. It is like the ocean. On the surface there are waves and surges, it is all dynamic movement, and down at the bottom it is peaceful. We cannot separate the waves from the tranquillity which is at the bottom. They have to go together. Dynamism and peace must go together. If some people feel that by doing Indian asanas they will get a peaceful feeling, they are correct. But again, by running and jumping and taking physical activities we can acquire dynamism; otherwise it will be all one-sided. So dynamism and tranquillity must go together, like the obverse and reverse of the same coin.

So in this philosophy are you creating something new, something different from what has been created generally in the East and in the West?

I do not want to say that I am creating something new. Only I am saying what the East and the West need to become complete and perfect. It is not my creation, only I am saying that I am aware of something and, if you see eye to eye with me, you will agree and, if you find it difficult to accept my theory, you are perfectly entitled to do so. I wish to say that the West has something to offer and the East has something to offer and their contributions are equally valuable.

I do not think that Western sports people in the past have considered that their sport would lead them to enlightenment!

No, I am not saying that. Sports only will help. We have to know how much importance we are giving to sports. Our goal is not to be the world's greatest athlete. Our goal is to have physical fitness and for that only the amount of sports—of running, jumping, throwing or tennis—that is necessary we shall do. Not to neglect the body as such is our aim.

If we pray and meditate soulfully, how can we neglect the body? It is one of the five members of our family—body, vital, mind, heart and soul. We shall pray with our heart, we shall meditate, and then, when activity is demanded of the body, we shall not neglect it. We have to give due importance to each member of our family. If we pay attention only to one member, then will the others not feel sad? If a father has five children, he has to pay attention to all the five.

Following are excerpts from an interview with John Hanc of New York Newsday, which took place on 19 November 1989.

How does running fit in with your teaching?

It perfectly fits in with our philosophy. Prayer and meditation always remind us of our inner running. The only difference between the outer running and the inner running is that in the inner running there is no set goal or destination. In the outer running, as soon as I have finished one hundred metres, let us say, the race is over. I may not win, but I have reached my goal. But in the inner running, we are Eternity's runner. Because we pray and meditate, we know that we have three friends: Eternity, Infinity and Immortality. Because we belong to Eternity, Infinity and Immortality, our journey is birthless and deathless; it has no beginning and no end. We have already started our journey and we are never going to end it. Along the way we may have certain temporary goals. But as soon as we reach these goals, they only become the starting point for new and higher goals.

Before we enter into the spiritual life, we want to possess the world. Our goal, let us say, is to become richer than the richest and to lord it over others like a Napoleon or Julius Caesar. Then gradually we come to realise that there is no satisfaction in this kind of life. We begin to reduce our material greed and diminish our desires. At the same time, we start trying to increase our positive qualities.

Take love, for example. As a child we start out by loving only our dear ones—the members of our immediate family. Then, after some time, we begin to claim the village where we were born as our own. Then we begin loving our district, our province, our country. But even this is not enough. At the United Nations all the nations are trying to become one. So we try to become citizens of the world and love the entire world. Like Socrates, we say, "I am not an Athenian or a Greek; I am a citizen of the world." So you see how much progress we can make in a positive way. This is our philosophy: anything that is bad—fear, doubt, anxiety, worry, suspicion and so on—we shall decrease, and anything that is good we shall increase. On the positive side, we shall start with an iota of love and expand it until it becomes universal love. There is no end to the amount of love we can have; we can keep expanding it until it encompasses not only God the Creation but also God the Creator, who is infinite. When we run in the inner world, we are running along the Road of Eternity, and we just continue, continue, continue.

The inner runner and the outer runner are like two brothers. The older, stronger brother can run a very long distance. But the younger one becomes tired after a certain distance because in the physical we are limited. Not only in the physical, but also in the mind and the vital we are limited. So after some time the outer brother takes rest and then he starts again—following the inner brother who is going on and on.

But even on the outer plane our capacity is constantly expanding. Right now 1300 miles is our longest race. To run 1300 miles in 18 days is almost beyond our imagination. We feel that is our ultimate capacity. But previously we felt that 1000 miles was the limit. Who thought of a 1300-mile race five years ago? At that time people would have thought I was a crazy man if I had suggested that. But now you see that this crazy man was right because people are doing it. Somebody just has to start. We always have to go ahead because life means progress.

The inner runner is always trying to inspire the outer runner. First the inner runner says, "Go forward, go forward, go ahead, go ahead!" Then the outer runner says, "How can I go ahead if you do not give me the aspiration and inner cry?" Then the inner runner gives the outer runner the inner cry to do something and to become something good. In this way the inner runner offers inspiration and aspiration to the outer runner.

While running, is it also a time to meditate?

For others I cannot speak, but in my case when I am jogging or walking, I am in a very high consciousness. At that time the world of thought ceases and I am in another world—not the thought-world but the world of self-giving and serving. While running, a runner is all joy unless he is suffering from muscle cramps or some other ailment or he is killing himself trying to become first. But in the New York Marathon, for example, thousands and thousands of people are running just for the joy of it. Even if they take five hours, no harm, so long as they finish. They say, "Every runner is a winner," and it is so true. This is also our philosophy.

You mentioned that when you first came up with the idea of 1300 miles, people said, "What kind of an idea is that?" What are you thinking about now? Have you got any other ideas?

I have other ideas. The only question is whether they can be fully manifested. We are not going to stop at 1300.* But before we go beyond that, the runners must acquire the inner confidence that they can do it. It is just like the idea of the marathon. In the beginning, only a handful of people ran the New York Marathon. At that time, people did not have the confidence. Now twenty or thirty thousand people are running it.

Does it give you joy to see the increasing number of runners who come to your races here?

It gives me joy not only when they come to our races but when they come to anybody's races. Everywhere in the world, if people can run, it will help them. One of our absolutely worst enemies is our lethargy. Early in the morning we do not want to get up. Then during the day we are not energetic; we are not inspired to do anything. But in the morning if we can energise ourselves with

---

*In 1996 the Sri Chinmoy Marathon Team organised a 2700 mile race, increased in 1997 to 3100 miles, which has been held yearly since then.

physical activities, then we can accomplish so many things during the rest of the day. That is why I say sports and physical fitness are of supreme importance. If we neglect the physical and let the body become weak, then the mind also becomes weak. At that time it does not have the strength to think of good things all the time and it starts to think of undivine things.

As a long-time athlete and observer of the sport of running, do you have any feelings about where the sport itself is going?

I am extremely happy that the running community is going out of its way to make sure the athletes do not take drugs. It is a great, great achievement. It is not only a physical or mental achievement; it is not only an achievement in the athletic world. It represents also a great advance for the spiritual life. People who take drugs are destroying their nerves and their health. God created us, so why are we destroying ourselves? We are like a flower in God's Heart-Garden. When we plant a seed, we watch it grow into a beautiful flower. The flower is our creation, and we get so much joy and delight from its beauty and fragrance. But if somebody grabs the flower and tears it to pieces, we will be very sad. Similarly, God is our Creator and He wants us to keep our body strong, our vital dynamic and our mind happy and peaceful.

Somebody may say, "No, it is my body, and I can do whatever I like with it. It is none of your business or anybody else's business what I do with my body." But that is not right. In a family, if right in front of you a brother or sister is taking drugs or becoming alcoholic, is it not your bounden duty to beg them to stop? They may say, "Mind your own business," but you will continue trying to persuade them to stop because you love them. Similarly, every human being is a member of our world-family. Because we claim others as part and parcel of our family, we will keep on trying to get them to do the right thing. If they do not listen, what can we do? But we will keep on trying.

I have seen you sitting and watching many of the Sri Chinmoy races. Many of the people running are not followers of yours, but they all seem to be having a good time.

I am very happy with the way my spiritual students have created such a good atmosphere for these people and are inspiring them in the running world. As I said, the world is all one family. We are inviting our brothers and sisters to come to our races, and it gives us joy when they participate. Our 1300-mile race is like a Thanksgiving Day celebration. Once a year the family comes together for Thanksgiving, and it gives us all such joy to see one another again.

On the ultra-distance side, you and the Sri Chinmoy Marathon Team have been leaders in expanding the limits of what people can run. Do you think there will be any limit to the distance people can run? Ten years from now will we be talking about a 2000-mile or a 5000-mile run?

There is no limit to the distance because there is no limit to human capacity. Human capacity depends on our inner hunger—how sincerely we need something or are crying for something. In the material world, if someone has tremendous greed and wants to become a multi-millionaire, he works very hard and eventually he fulfils his desire. But by possessing the material world, we can never be happy. We can only find joy by serving as an instrument of God and fulfilling His Will. If God wants us to be a sprinter or an ultramarathon runner and if we follow His Dictates, then naturally we will become very happy. It will not matter if we stand first or last. Success or failure we shall place at His Feet. What matters is that we are pleasing God in His own Way. How do we know what God wants us to do? By praying and meditating.

If it is God's Will for us to do something, there is absolutely no limit to human capacity. One of my students from Washington,

D.C. [Suprabha Beckjord] is thinner than the thinnest. If you see her, it will be beyond your imagination that she can run 1000 miles. But she does it. Because of her aspiration and heart's cry, God is supplying her with Grace from Above in the form of inner energy and strength.

In my case, I have lifted heavy weights. In a year's time I have also lifted 1300 people using only one arm. Many of them were heavier than I am. I have even lifted two people at once, although I am fifty-four years old and my muscles are smaller than the smallest. How is it possible? I have a mind, and I am the first person to disbelieve it. But through God's Grace, it is possible.

On 10 December 1989, freelance journalist Mark Teich interviewed Sri Chinmoy in preparation for an article for Sports Illustrated *magazine. Following are excerpts from the interview.*

How did you become involved in ultra-distance running? I know you were a sprinter as a youth, but when did you fall in love with ultra-distance running?

About twelve years ago. For physical fitness, I feel that long distance is better for most people than sprinting. One out of a thousand, or even one out of ten thousand can be a sprinter, whereas thousands of people can run long distance daily. Also, long distance running reminds us of our inner life. It makes us feel that we are running along Eternity's Road. Each individual is a pilgrim. We are all pilgrims, and it is our bounden duty to walk, march and run along Eternity's Road. When we run long distances, we are reminded of our inner life. At the same time, long distance runners receive many good things from Above: patience, consecration and a self-disciplined and dedicated life.

Every day long distance runners spend half an hour, an hour or two hours running and, while running, they receive special blessings from Mother Earth, from nature. They are breathing fresh air.

They are enjoying the fragrance of flowers and the blessings from the trees and so forth, whereas short-distance sprinters run on the track. There they deal with speed, speed, speed. They try to run fast, faster, fastest. They have no time to enjoy the beauty of nature or to receive the blessings of Mother Earth.

As a sprinter, I know a little bit about sprinting, and I saw that very few of my disciples are blessed with speed. But easily they can develop stamina and endurance by practising long-distance running for a few months. Also, for inner tranquillity, I feel that long-distance running is far, far better than sprinting.

An ultramarathon is very much a kind of inner search, as opposed to competitive sports like football. Is that what you find attractive?

Outwardly you can say that. But, as I said before, I received inspiration from within. Running long distance is like being part of a family—thousands of people are going together. Sprinting is a matter of a single individual, all by himself in a lane. He cannot come out of his lane, otherwise he will be disqualified or there will be a real accident.

In long distance, the runners are going slowly and steadily towards their goal, and there is constant joy. In the New York Marathon, they say that every runner is a winner. This slogan I admire very much—every runner is a winner. Already the champions have finished, and we are cheerfully going on, ten miles behind them. Then, when we come to the finish, the organisers console us and inspire us by saying that every runner is a winner.

In the spiritual life also, everybody is a winner—provided you do not give up. If you give up, you are not a winner. Slow and steady wins the race. Everybody cannot have the same capacity, the same standard. You will go according to your speed, and I will go according to my speed. If you and I can maintain our cheerfulness and reach our destination, it does not matter whether you arrive first or I arrive first. We are both winners because we are competing with ourselves on the strength of our faith in ourselves and in God.

I have been reading some of your writings on running, as well as some things on meditation. In one talk that you gave before the New York Marathon a few years ago, you told your students to run their best, but if they happen not to run their best time, if they fail in their personal expectations, not to worry about that at all. You said the main thing was their cheerfulness, that the running itself was the most important thing. I also know that you do have a special respect for champions like Carl Lewis. Can you reconcile these two attitudes for me?

Both ideas can easily go together. I appreciate athletes like Carl Lewis and other world champions because I feel that they are a great manifestation of God. Let us take running as a garden. One rose may be most beautifully blossomed. Again, there are also many little buds. So I tell the little buds, "If you are not blossomed fully today, do not worry. Only pray to God to let His Will be done in and through you. And if you are cheerful, you will receive more inspiration, more aspiration."

Let us say I wanted to run the marathon in four hours and I complete the distance in four and a half hours. If I am doomed to disappointment, tomorrow I may not go out to run, I may even give up running. But if I cheerfully accept the result, then I will receive added strength. Today I have failed to achieve my goal, but failures, as you know, are the pillars of success.

Hundreds of times I failed to lift 300 pounds with one arm. But I continued, and afterwards I went on to lift much heavier weights. Our philosophy is never to give up. If we give up, how can we continue? And if we do not continue, how can we maintain our cheerfulness? To all my students I say, "Remain cheerful, no matter what the results." We are spiritual people. We know that it is our bounden duty to offer the results of what we do to God. He has given us the capacity to run. It is He who is running in and through us. So let us offer our gratitude to God.

Carl Lewis and other super-excellent stars in various walks of life we take as members of our family. Being spiritual seekers, we feel that the whole world is ours—not in the sense of possessing the world, but in the sense of embracing the world. You, he and I are all one. So if some member of the family does something, we feel it is our bounden duty to appreciate that person.

It is all one world. For my weightlifting programme, I have given the name "Lifting Up the World with a Oneness-Heart." Carl Lewis perfectly fits in with us. So do Roberta Flack, Narada Michael Walden, Bill Pearl and countless others. They are all members of our family. They love us and we love them. When a member of our family does something good, we feel it is our duty to appreciate and admire that person. In this way, we increase his capacity. Mutual appreciation is the right thing.

To those who are not champions, I say, "You do your very best, and place the results at the Feet of God." To those who are champions, if they do not do well at a particular time, I say, "Do not be disappointed! Do not give up!"

When somebody like Stu Mittelman or Yiannis Kouros or Fred Lebow says, "You know, if Sri Chinmoy were not doing this now, nobody would be doing it," it is very impressive. They say it would be a huge loss if you ever stopped conducting these races. You do not respond to that at all? In other words, you might stop the events when your Inner Pilot told you to stop them, even if it meant the end of the ultramarathon?

This Creation is not mine. It is God's Creation. Again, I am absolutely sure that God does not want anything that is good to disappear from His Creation. Today He has inspired me to serve ultra-distance running. But if He sees that I am not doing well, or if He has had enough experiences in and through me, then He can easily choose another instrument.

But I am absolutely sure that God will not ask human beings to give up long distance running. "Run and become, become and run"—this is the motto of our Sri Chinmoy Marathon Team. Something that is good in God's Creation will always last; it will only make progress. From time to time we may see setbacks, but eventually it is bound to flourish.

The following is an interview with the St. Louis Post-Dispatch *that took place on 27 June 1987 prior to the opening ceremony of the first US National Senior Olympics. Sri Chinmoy was invited to lead the opening meditation at that event and to address the audience.*

As a truth-seeker and a God-lover, I feel the supreme necessity of physical fitness. To me, the body is the temple, and inside the temple is the shrine. If there is no temple, then there can be no shrine. The shrine is our soul, our inner life, our inner hunger for truth, for delight, for beauty, for perfection. The body and the soul must go together, like the inner life and the outer life. If I have a good thought inside my mind, then I can express it to the world at large. If I have a pure heart, then in my outer actions and dealings also, I will be pure. The inner and the outer must go together. This is my simple philosophy.

Which comes first—the inner life or the outer life?

God always comes first. The Creation did not create God. God is both God the Creator and God the Creation. Then they become one, inseparably one. But we have to say the Vision of God came first, then the manifestation of God. The manifestation cannot come before the vision. You envision something and then you try to give shape and form to it. So the Vision of God came before the manifestation of God.

The physical strength or physical capacity that we have is the result of our inner aspiration. That is to say, how we behave inwardly is of supreme importance at the beginning, and then how we behave and react in our outer life. Our inner life of aspiration must come first; then comes our outer life of dedication. They go together, but the one will lead and guide the other. If we are not guided by our inner thoughts, inner goodwill, inner strength, then we will be nowhere in the outer life.

How do exercise and competition help the inner life?

In my case, I use the term 'self-transcendence'. I do not compete with anybody. I compete with myself. It is like a seed that germinates and becomes a plant. Then it becomes a tree and, finally, it grows into a huge banyan tree. I always try to transcend myself. In the weightlifting world, I started lifting 40 pounds with one arm and then I went up and up.

There are many athletes who get inspiration and enthusiasm only when they compete with others. I cannot blame them. If someone is in a position to compete with somebody else, that means he is inspired, he is enthusiastic. If he is competing with someone, then he can bring to the fore his utmost capacity. Otherwise he may be lethargic. He may not practise daily. The physical discipline in his life may come into existence only when he knows that he has to compete with somebody else. Otherwise, he may not take these physical exercises seriously.

But with God's Grace, I practise daily for physical fitness and at the same time I try to better myself, I try to improve my capacity.

Is improvement and building on previous records important, or is the main thing to exercise daily?

I feel improvement is necessary in order for us to make progress. In this world we are happy only when we make progress. When I studied English, in the beginning I had to learn the alphabet, the ABC's. Now at this age, if I had not studied hundreds and thousands of English books, I would have felt miserable because my teacher taught me the ABC's so many years ago. So that is called progress. This progress is giving me satisfaction. But if we are complacent and we do not want to go forward, then we will not be happy.

Again, we have to know that there is a great difference between competition and progress. When we want to compete with others, sometimes we adopt foul means—by hook or by crook we try to win. Then we bring to the fore our feelings of rivalry and almost animal propensities, animal qualities. We are only thinking of how we can defeat others, how we can lord it over others. But when we are competing with ourselves, we know that we have to purify our inner existence in order to improve. So here is the difference. When it is a matter of self-transcendence, we have to depend on our inner purity, inner love, vastness and oneness with the rest of the world. We try to develop universal goodwill, whereas, while competing with others, we may not have those feelings. At that time, we may see others as rivals, we are on the border of enmity with them. It can be as if we are fighting with enemies when we are competing. But when we are trying to transcend ourselves, we cannot fight with ourselves. If we can go ten steps ahead today, tomorrow we will try to cover twenty steps, and the day after thirty steps.

Spiritually, what can we get from games? Volleyball, for instance, is one of those sports that they will be doing in the Senior Olympics.

Very good. I happened to be a volleyball player in my teens. I was the captain, the main instructor, in the place where I was brought up in India, for many, many years. I used to play volleyball quite well.

From the spiritual point of view, there are many things we can learn from games. One is fellow feeling. Then, in volleyball there is something called a serve. Let us take the term 'serve'. By playing, we are serving mankind. You will say, "How?" Let us say you are playing volleyball, and I am in the audience. You are giving me joy and inspiration. You are playing so well, you are smashing the ball and doing all kinds of things.

Why do we watch sports? The world needs inspiration and enthusiasm. You play volleyball extremely well, and I am inspired by it. Then I go and play tennis. You have given me the inspiration, and I go and play some other game. But you gave me the joy, you gave me the inspiration, you gave me the courage. Like that, each person can get inspiration from another person to do better in their own respective fields.

In your remarks tonight, what do you anticipate saying to the Senior Olympians?

I only wish to encourage them and inspire them. I will tell them that they have developed wisdom. I use the term 'wisdom-light'. These senior athletes do not belong to the fleeting time. They belong to Time eternal. They are running along Eternity's Road, challenging the giant pride of self-doubt. Self-doubt so proudly declares, "I cannot do this, I cannot do that." The giant pride of self-doubt stands against us in the battlefield of life. These Senior Olympians are challenging their own self-doubt. They are shaking hands smilingly and proudly with impossibility. People say, "It is impossible—a person of that age cannot do pole-vault. They cannot do shot-put or hurdles." But these Senior Olympians are proving that there is no such thing as impossibility.

What is the relationship between meditation and sports? I know in martial arts, which is something I've done for many years, there is a direct relationship, but does it also exist with sports?

In sports we need energy, strength and dynamism. When we meditate, we make our mind calm and quiet. If inside us there is peace, then we will derive tremendous strength from our inner life. That is to say, if I have a peaceful moment, even for one second, that peace will come to me as solid strength in my sports, whether I am running or jumping or throwing. That strength is almost indomitable strength, whereas if we are restless, we do not have strength like that.

Look at an elephant. An elephant has tremendous strength. It is not restless like a monkey which is moving here and there. It is exactly the same for us. In our inner life if we have the strength of an elephant, then only in our outer life can we be peaceful. A lion is very peaceful. Then when something happens, he starts roaring. But its strength is the peace that it has. It has confidence. But a monkey and other animals that are very, very restless, what kind of strength do they have? Meditation gives us inner strength. Once we have inner strength, we are bound to be successful in our outer life.

>
> **Just silence the mind.**
> **Lo!**
> **Cosmic energy enters**
> **Into our entire being,**
> **And tremendous energy**
> **Flows in and through us.**

>
> **How can you get more energy?**
> **Only by challenging**
> **What is dissatisfying you**
> **Inside yourself.**

Without daring
And without enduring,
There can be no
Appreciable outer success
And laudable inner progress.

When I am weak,
I think of others'
Capacities.
When I am strong,
I think of my own
Yet unnoticed
Capacities.

10
THE INNER RUNNER

The outer running reminds us that a higher, deeper,
more illumining and more fulfilling goal
is ahead of us in the inner world.

The Inner Running and the Outer Running

Spiritual people often like running because it reminds them of their inner journey. The outer running reminds them that a higher, deeper, more illumining and more fulfilling goal is ahead of them in the inner world, and for that reason running gives them real joy.

Each individual on earth is running towards his Destination. If the runner is simple, he will wear only the basic garments that are necessary. He will not wear something very heavy or expensive to draw the attention of the spectators. If the runner is sincere, then he will run in his own lane. He will not enter into the lanes of others and thus disturb them and create confusion in them. If the runner is pure, then in silence he will conquer the spectators' hearts. So by being simple, sincere and pure he will run the fastest. Not only will he run the fastest, but while he is running there will come a time when he will feel that the goal itself has been within his easy reach right from the beginning.

> **Your days of excellence-joys**
> **Are ahead of you**
> **And**
> **Not behind you.**
> **Why, then, do you not**
> **Immediately run and declare:**
> **"The goal is won!"?**

We run the fastest when we do not look to this side or that side. If we let ourselves become distracted by thinking of the person who is either beside us or behind us but not at the goal itself, we will fail to reach the goal. We are running towards the goal for peace, light and bliss. Since we cannot get these things from the imperfect person we are thinking of, why should we waste our time thinking of him? Always think of the goal and your problem will be solved.

> He was a great runner.
> In the outer world he ran
>> To satisfy his quenchless thirst
>> For name and fame.
> In the inner world he ran
>> To feed and satisfy
>> The God-hunger in him.

How long it takes to reach the goal depends on how fast you run. If you are a slow runner it will take you forty or fifty seconds to run one hundred metres. But a first-class runner will do it in eleven seconds because he has the capacity to run faster. If someone has the eagerness to learn from a coach or an instructor, naturally he will run the fastest. But if somebody does not practise or take instruction from the coach, then how will he run as fast as someone who does? So speed is of utmost importance. In the case of running a race, it is a matter of ten or twenty or thirty seconds. But in the case of the spiritual life, it is a matter of ten or twenty or forty or sixty incarnations. If you run the fastest when a spiritual Master enters into your life, at that time you have a golden opportunity. All spiritual Masters have said that when spiritual figures descend, they are like an oceanliner that can carry many people very fast.

> Inspiration I need
> To run my race.
> Aspiration I need
> To win my race.
> Realisation I need
> To feel God's Grace.

The marathon race is more than twenty-six miles long. At the moment the starter fires the gun, if the runner thinks that after twenty-six miles he will reach the goal, he will be totally disgusted. "I have to run twenty-six miles!" he will think; then he will just give up. No, while he is running, he has to think that he is covering a quarter mile, a half mile, a mile, and so on. If he thinks that he has to reach the goal all at once, the moment he starts, he will be disheartened. He will say it is impossible. If a kindergarten student thinks of his Master's degree while he is learning the alphabet, then it is impossible. If he thinks he has to get his Master's degree as soon as possible, he will just go crazy. But if he feels that now he is in kindergarten, tomorrow he will be in primary school, then high school and so on, then he will have constant inspiration.

> Always take one more step
> Than you intended to.
> You can, without fail, do it.
> Lo, you have done it.

Each soul is running consciously or unconsciously towards the Goal, but those who are running consciously will reach the Goal sooner than those who are still asleep.

Each individual has left the starting point. One individual may be behind another in the Godward race, but all are running towards the same goal. Each individual is progressing.

God always wants us to move ahead; He does not want us to look back. We know that while a runner is running fast, if he looks back, he will stumble. Similarly, if we are constantly looking behind at the year that we are leaving aside, we will think of our sorrow, misery, frustration, failure and so forth. But if we look forward, we will see hope dawning deep within us. Every day in this New Year is equally important. Suppose the runner has to run one hundred metres to reach the goal. After covering twenty metres at top speed, he feels that since he is running so fast, he is going to reach the goal in a second. So, relaxation comes. But once the starter has fired the gun, if the runner from the beginning to the end maintains top speed, then only is he able to win the race.

When we aspire to achieve a life-goal, we progress gradually. But during this gradual process, we have to maintain the same type of aspiration. Suppose a runner is going to run five miles. When the starter fires the gun, the runner is inspired and he begins running very fast. But after two or three miles, he becomes very tired. Running becomes tedious and difficult. If the runner gives up running just because he is tired and because his inspiration is gone, he does not reach his goal. But if he continues running, he will finally reach the goal. Then he will definitely feel that it was worth the struggle and suffering of the body.

Every day, when morning dawns, we should feel that we have something new to accomplish. If we are aspiring, we are always in the process of running. When we start our journey in the morning, we should feel that today is the continuation of yesterday's journey; we should not take it as a totally new beginning. And tomorrow we should feel that we have travelled still another mile. Then, we know one day that we will reach our Goal. Even if our speed decreases, we have to continue running and not give up on the way. When we reach our Goal, we will see that it was worth the struggle.

Self-transcendence
Is my
Ever-blossoming goal.

Why is my aspiration lower in the morning?

Your aspiration is not low in the morning. Think of a runner. Some runners have a slow start when the starter fires the gun, but in a few minutes' time they speed up. So you can say that you have a poor start, but in a few seconds or a few hours you speed up. You may ask why. Perhaps the previous evening you were not concentrating on the determination-aspect of your life. The determination-aspect you get when you concentrate on the navel area and bring the life-energy upwards. From the navel it has to go to the heart and then, from the heart, you bring it to the head. It should pass through the crown centre. From the navel it has to go up, and then you get tremendous determination.

In your case, do not worry if the start is slow, as long as you can pick up the speed. Sometimes people have a very good start and after ten metres they collapse. They can not keep up the same speed. But if you have a slow start and then during the whole day if you can run very fast, it is wonderful. But if you want to have a very good start and also maintain the same speed, then concentrate on the navel and bring the life-energy upwards. Then you will have tremendous energy and the following day you will have a very good meditation.

Is there a way to aspire even while you are relaxing?

There is a special way. A runner, for example, prepares himself for some time before he takes a start. Then, he starts and gradually increases his speed, and after a few moments his co-ordination becomes perfect. Then, he can relax in his co-ordination and still not lose his speed. Similarly, if the preparation is good and the start is good and the forward movement is speeding ahead satisfactorily, then one will be able to keep one's aspiration intact even with inner relaxation.

Meditation

Meditation is like running. If you run stiffly, you get nowhere. You must be relaxed; the body has to be relaxed. But if you go to the extreme, then you become complacent.

So a beginner has to sit in a quiet place, keeping the backbone erect and trying to breathe quietly and slowly and focussing the attention either on the third eye between the eyebrows, or on the heart centre. A beginner has to go through all kinds of discipline. I did it. One cannot be a good runner overnight; it takes time. When one becomes a good runner, everything—his hand movements, his leg movements—is perfectly co-ordinated.

You should concentrate for a few minutes each day before entering into meditation. You are like a runner who has to clear the track—see if there are any obstacles and then remove them. Then when you begin meditating, feel that you are running very fast, with all obstacles out of your way. You are like an express train that only stops when you reach the Goal. This is the last stage, contemplation.

If you feel that you cannot meditate for half an hour, no harm. Meditate for ten minutes. Then you will feel, "Oh, only ten minutes. Easily I can do that." If your goal is very limited, then you will give it all your energy. If it is two hours, you may feel that to keep running at the same speed is impossible. But if it is ten minutes, anybody can meditate for ten minutes. So, first you relax yourself with the idea that the goal is within reach. If you have to run twenty miles, then you are scared to death. But if you see that the goal is within sight, then you say, "Oh, I am seeing it. Let me run."

If you want to meditate well for fifteen minutes, try to keep aside one hour for your meditation. Then consider forty-five minutes as being only for your preparation. Again, you may feel that if you sit down for fifteen minutes, you will be able to meditate well and you will not need forty-five minutes extra. You may feel that you do not have to take a few preliminary starts before you run the race.

Before a sprinter runs the full distance of one hundred metres, he runs twenty or thirty metres in order to warm up, so that his body can be properly co-ordinated. So the same principle can be applied here. If it is necessary, we shall take a few practice starts. And if it is not necessary, then right away we shall cover the 100-metre distance—that is to say, we shall go deep within.

In the spiritual life we have to go very slowly, steadily and unerringly. When we meditate, we have to know how long we can meditate soulfully, either five minutes or ten minutes or fifteen minutes or twenty minutes. If I know that my capacity is to run 100 metres, then I will run 100 metres for a few days or a few months. But if I have the capacity to run only 100 metres and all of a sudden I want to run 400 metres, then naturally I will collapse. I will complete it with greatest difficulty and then I will fall down.

When I feel something flowing in my meditation, I become complacent. Should I try to work harder at it?

At the start of a race when the judge says, "On your mark, get set, go!" there is so much alertness and tension. Then, after covering thirty metres, your arms and your legs get a kind of co-ordination. At that time you feel that you are totally relaxed, that you are not running at all. But your speed is in no way slower; it is still very fast. Just because your mind is not convincing you that you are making some unusual effort, you imagine that you are not running fast enough. But it is not true.

When I do my paintings or write poetry, at that time I go very fast. But I am totally relaxed while I am doing it. So when you are doing something, do not think of the start. At the time of the start, alertness, eagerness, indecision, tension, fear and doubt all come and make you feel that you are doing something. Then, once you have started, these forces leave you. At that time you are in the process of completing your journey. If you think of the start, you will only make a comparison between the start and the point halfway through the race. But this is a mistake. When you are at the halfway mark, only try to reach the goal. Look ahead and do not think of the thing that you did before.

> **Run, run, with your soul's**
> **Dynamism-river-flow.**
> **You are bound to succeed**
> **In everything that you want to do**
> **And everything that you want to become.**

Whoever can
Soulfully and powerfully smile
The oneness-smile
Before the game,
During the game
And after the game
Is undoubtedly
The real winner.

11
RUNNING AND THE LIFE-GAME

In the life-game, each soul is running
consciously or unconsciously
towards the goal of inner perfection.

Life and sports cannot be separated; they are one. As a matter of fact, life itself is a game. This game can be played extremely well, provided the player develops consciously or unconsciously the capacity to invoke the transcendental energy which is always manifested in action.

In the life-game, each soul is running consciously or unconsciously towards the Goal of inner perfection. There is not a single individual who has not left the starting point. Now, one individual may be behind another in the Godward race, but all are making progress and running towards the same goal.

When you enter into the spiritual life, it means that you have consciously begun your inner journey. If you are running consciously, then naturally you will reach the Goal sooner than those who are still asleep. There are many reasons why you may be inspired to consciously run towards the Goal. You may be inspired to run towards the Goal because you see so many others who are also running, and this makes you feel that the Goal has something to offer.

Again, you may want to run towards the Goal because you yourself have an intense inner cry. Your inner cry for truth and light and love has increased; so you are running towards the Goal. Why is it that in you the inner cry has increased, whereas others are still fast asleep? It is because God has inspired you. It is not that you just come out of your house and decide to run. No, something within you, an inner urge, inspires you to go out and run. And who has given you that inner urge if not our Beloved Supreme?

Spirituality is a one-way road that leads you to your Goal. Once you have embarked on your journey, you cannot go back. The starting point is gone. Once evolution starts on any plane, you cannot go back to the initial point.

If you are consciously running towards the Goal, then naturally you want to get there sooner than the soonest. If you want to run fast, faster, fastest, then you have to simplify your outer life, your life of confusion, your life of desire, your life of anxiety and worry. At the same time, you have to intensify your inner life, your life of aspiration, your life of dedication and illumination.

Sometimes when you see your Goal in front of you, you think that you should be able to reach it at once, although you may be a little tired. You are tired because your capacity is limited. Nevertheless, your mind wants to just grab the Goal. But there is a limit to how fast you can go. Like a runner, you must be careful not to fall just before you reach the finishing line.

Again, you can say that there is no such thing as a fall. Since there is only one road, one way to the Goal, it is not possible to fall off the path. It is just that sometimes you take rest or halt for a while. But no matter how long you rest, or how slowly you go, you cannot fall off the path. Purification and illumination are bound to take place at God's choice Hour. At that time, first you will see that the Goal is right in front of you. Then you will feel that the Goal is within you, and finally you will come to realise that not only is the Goal within you, but you are the Goal itself. Your own higher self is the Goal that your lower self has been searching for.

> **Try to be a runner
> And try all the time
> To surpass and go beyond
> All that is bothering you
> And standing in your way.**

The Outer Running and the Inner Running

The outer running is a powerful struggle for a great independence. The inner running is a soulful cry for a good interdependence. Independence brings to the fore what we have unmistakably deep within: a freedom-smile. Interdependence makes us conscious of what we eternally are: a oneness-satisfaction.

The outer running is a burning desire to achieve everything that we see here on earth. The inner running is a climbing aspiration to receive from Above a vast compassion-sky and to give from below a tiny gratitude-flame.

The outer running is an extraordinary success on the mountain-summit. The inner running is an exemplary progress along Eternity's sunlit Road. Success is the ready and immediate acceptance of the challenges from difficulties untold. Progress is the soulful and grateful acceptance of the blessingful joy from prosperities unfathomed.

The outer runner and the inner runner: two aspects of the seeker-runner. The outer runner does; therefore, he succeeds. The inner runner becomes; therefore, he proceeds. When he succeeds, the seeker-runner gets a new name: glorification. When he proceeds, the seeker-runner gets a new name: illumination.

The seeker-runner's glorification is a beautiful flower that charms and inspires his entire life. The seeker-runner's illumination is a fruitful tree that shelters and nourishes his entire earthly existence.

The outer running is a colossal satisfaction, although at times it may be quite oblivious to the existence-reality of a quiet perfection. The inner running is a perpetual satisfaction in and through a blossoming perfection.

The seeker-runner has a shadowless dream of his full realisation-day in his outer running. The seeker-runner has a sleepless vision of his God's full Manifestation-Hour in his inner running.

The outer runner challenges the Himalayan pride of impossibility. The inner runner smilingly arranges a feast not only with impossibility but also with Immortality.

The outer runner runs through the golden gate and arrives at the sound-kingdom. The inner runner enters into the unique palace, runs up to its highest floor and places himself at the very Feet of the Silence-King.

Finally, the seeker-runner's outer running says to his inner running, "Look, I am giving you what I now have: my majesty's crown." The seeker-runner's inner running says to his outer running, "Look, I am giving you what I now am: my beauty's throne."

> The outer running may not make
> The mind less doubtful,
> But it may temporarily reduce
> The mind´s capacity
> To think undivine thoughts.

We Run, We Become

We run. We become. We run in the outer world. We become in the inner world. We run to succeed. We become to proceed.

In the spiritual life, speed is of paramount importance. In the outer world, speed is founded mostly upon inspiration. In the inner world, speed is founded mostly upon aspiration.

Inspiration helps us run—far, farther, farthest. It helps us run the length and breadth of the world. Aspiration helps us become—fast, faster, fastest—the chosen instrument of our Beloved Supreme.

Inspiration tells us to look around and thus feel and see boundless light, energy and power. Aspiration tells us to dive deep within and enjoy boundless inner nectar and delight.

Inspiration tells us to claim and proclaim our own divinity, which is our birthright. Aspiration tells us to feel and realise once and for all that we are exact prototypes of our Beloved Supreme and thus we can be as great, as good, as divine and as perfect as He is.

Inspiration tells us to become our true selves. Aspiration tells us to become God Himself.

Inspiration tells us to feel what we soulfully have: God's Love, God's Compassion, God's Beauty and God's Peace in infinite measure. Aspiration tells us to feel at every moment that we are of the Source and for the Source. We are of our Beloved Supreme the One and we are for our Beloved Supreme the many. Him to fulfil, Him to manifest, Him to satisfy unconditionally in His own Way is the reason we have taken human birth.

We run. We become. At every moment we are running to become something great, sublime, divine and supreme. While we are becoming, we feel that we are in the process of reaching our ultimate Goal. But today's Goal is only the starting point for tomorrow's new dawn. At every moment we are transcending our previous achievements; we are transcending what we have and what we are. By virtue of our self-giving, we are becoming the Beauty, the Light and the Delight of our Beloved Supreme.

A Great Champion

A great champion is he who wins all the races.

A great champion is he who participates in all the races.

A great champion is he who does not care for the results of the races—whether he is first or last or in between. He races just to get joy and give joy to the observers.

A great champion is he who transcends his own previous records.

A great champion is he who maintains his standard.

A great champion is he who remains happy even when he cannot maintain his standard.

A great champion is he who has established his inseparable oneness with the winner and the loser alike.

A great champion is he who, owing to the advancement of years, retires from racing or terminates his career happily and cheerfully.

A great champion is he who longs to see the fulfilment of his dreams—if not through himself, then in and through others. It does not even have to be in and through his own dear ones; it can be in and through any human being on earth. If someone who could not manifest his own dreams is extremely happy when he sees his vision being manifested into reality through somebody else, then he is a really great champion.

A great champion is he who meditates on his Inner Pilot for the fulfilment of His Will before the race, during the race and after the race.

A great champion is he who sees and feels that he is a mere instrument of his Inner Pilot and that his Inner Pilot is racing in and through him, according to his own capacity of receptivity.

A champion of champions is he whose inner life has become the Vision of his Absolute Supreme and whose outer life has become the perfection-channel of his Beloved Supreme.

> **Greatness**
> **Is a matter of a moment.**
> **Goodness**
> **Is the work of a lifetime.**

12
MY DAILY RUNNING EXPERIENCES

"We have to prove that mind can win over matter.
But unfortunately, today matter has won!"

One day while running, I was talking to myself in Bengali, in my Chittagong dialect: "I cannot go any farther."

What could I do? I was dying! I kept saying, "I will not be able to go any farther."

Then, a child about eight years old came up to me and said, "Don't talk. It will make you more exhausted. Don't talk."

5 December 1978

Last night, after six and a half miles, I was returning at one-thirty in the morning near the Grand Central Parkway. A car came slowly towards me. I was going away, but it went right against the red light. I said, "O God, what is he doing?"

The driver was smoking and his wife was sitting beside him. The man leaned out the window and said to me, "Please come near me. I won't harm you. You don't have to be afraid." It was a very respectable looking couple, so I went over to the car. The man said, "Tell me, why are you running at this hour?"

I said, "I like it, I enjoy it."

The man said to his wife, "Every day I also run at this hour and you call me crazy. Now, here is somebody else who is running."

The lady said, "Yes, another crazy fellow like you!" Then she said to me, "Young man, go home and sleep. If you don't sleep, you will die soon. But if you don't run, you are not going to die soon."

The man said, "It is better to die sooner than to live with a wife like you."

The lady pushed her husband and knocked his cigarette out of his mouth. It fell down on the street, coming very close to my leg. But fortunately it did not hit me.

I started laughing, and then both of them started laughing and laughing. Finally they said to me, "Thanks a lot."

15 August 1979

When I went out running I saw a short, thin, old man with a hat and cane sitting on the edge of a wall, waiting for the bus. I did not pay any attention to him, but when I came back from my seven-mile run, the same old man was still waiting there. He said to me, "How I wish I could get back my youth."

I said, "I, too, miss my youth."

"How old are you?" asked the man.

"Forty-eight," I answered.

"I am seventy-three," said the man.

I stayed there with him for two or three minutes and then I finished my run. *3 September 1979*

Yesterday when I was finishing a six-mile run on 150th Street, a young boy came up to me and said, "Nice style, but you need longer strides."

He began demonstrating, saying that after each stride I should pause and press the ground with my toes. "In this way your stride becomes longer."

He was very nice and demonstrated this for two minutes or so. I did not tell him that I know all the different stride techniques.

21 September 1979

At four in the afternoon, after running a half-mile, I stopped for two seconds in front of an old man, an invalid who was sitting in a wheelchair in front of his house.

He said to me, "Don't stop, don't stop! It's not allowed. Keep going, keep going. Don't stop, it's not allowed."

I thanked him, and then I ran a mile and a half. When I was returning, I thought that the old man would still be there and give me the same advice. So about 100 metres before his house, I stopped for a few seconds and thought of him. Immediately I saw a flash and heard him say in the inner world, "That's perfect."

When I saw him 100 metres later, I smiled and he said, "That's perfect." He did not know that I had stopped 100 metres before.

26 September 1979

When I had run a mile and a half, I stopped for a second or two. Immediately a tiny dog came and sat by my right foot, wanting me to caress it and give it a little kindness. I never do this kind of thing, but this time I bent a little to touch the dog's head. The owner, who was bald-headed, wearing a grey coat, came over to me and said, "My Dolly has fallen in love with you."

I kept caressing the dog. The owner said, "Dolly, do you want to become a great runner like this gentleman?"

I said, "How I wish I could become a great runner!"

29 September 1979

When I was running the day before yesterday, I felt such tiredness in my body. The body was so undivine, not receptive at all. After 200 metres, I stopped for no rhyme or reason. After 400 metres, again I stopped. This time I got mad at myself. "Is it tiredness or is it something else?" I asked.

Inwardly I said a few times, "I am not going to stop, I am not going to stop." Then I began chanting out loud, at every step, "No, never! No, never! No, never!" In this way I covered one mile. If people had heard me chanting in the street, they would have said: "Insane!" Luckily, no one was around. Then I ran all the way back home, feeling quite happy.

29 September 1979

The day before the Phidippides Marathon in Athens, I took a cab and went to the marathon starting point. I was disappointed, frightened, to say the least, when I saw the whole course.

I said, "Since I came all the way, best thing is to die on the battlefield."

But when you are in the car, the battlefield is not a real battlefield. Only when you start running, when you are on the ground, is it a real battlefield.

When I saw it in the car, I still had a little hope that I would be able to manage it. Secretly I had a little hope that I would be able to finish it. Alas, the actual day was something else!

As soon as I reached five and a half miles, I saw the first hill. For at least 1,200 metres it went up. It was not yet six miles, so still I had strength.

The next 200 metres were not downhill but flat, and then again it went up for practically half a mile. Next it went down—this time not even for 100 metres—and again up.

Like this, when I came to nine miles, I felt miserable. I said, "What am I going to do?" Luckily, at that time it went downhill for about 800 metres. I was so delighted, so happy; at last there was an oasis in the desert.

Alas, after 800 metres it went up again.

From five and a half miles it started, and for the next fourteen miles it was only hills. And you will not believe me, but there were no downhills. At most it would be flat for 100 or 200 metres and then it went up, up, up. There were three hills that were at least, at least, one mile long.

People were cursing and dying. One young man was lying right on the street—not on the sidewalk but right on the street—massaging his knee and saying, "Never in this lifetime will I run again." Terrible! Terrible!

Some were running fifty metres and walking fifty metres. You will not believe it, but three elderly men were walking faster than I could run. I was running and they were walking, but my running was not as good as their walking.

One of them was mischievous enough to laugh at me. He was laughing at me because I was running and he was beating me while walking. But after two miles I saw him; he had become so tired that he went to drink ERG or water, and he did not appear for a long time.

At eighteen miles my first attack came: my hamstring revolted. When it was twenty-one miles, out of the blue, five songs I heard all at once. It was absolutely a chorus; the music was on! How can I get five cramps at a time? The pain was excruciating. I was helpless, flat, dead! Some of my students were helping me. One of them was seated and, with a sponge, was pressing my leg with cold water, while another was pushing my toes forward. How hard, how quickly, the first one was massaging me! And afterwards, four or five times he did it again. Even now it frightens me when I think of the pain—excruciating!

After that experience I started walking. Slower than the slowest, a quarter mile I walked. Again the pain, so again I walked.

Running is forbidden now. Just walk, walk as slowly as possible. When it was twenty-three miles, another new friend came—right here in the neck. I could not breathe in; neither nostril was functioning.

This was really unbearable! With the previous pain, at least I was able to breathe in, so I felt that there was something going on. But when it started in this muscle, I was not able to breathe even. Too much, too much!

Some people—I think, nurses—came up, but we did not take their help. I said, "I have got my help."

When it was twenty-five miles, a strong desire arose: "Oh, let me run at least the last mile." It was a desire, nothing else. As soon as I tried, all the cramps said to me, "Where are you going? We are still alive." Such pain!

I thought 800 metres, 400 metres, 100 metres I would run. Finally, when it was only twenty metres, the officials were asking me to run. I tried, but I knew if I had run, I would have dropped right there and fainted, so I just dragged myself. I was not even walking—just dragging my body. Anyway, I managed to finish.

The management of the race was far from perfection. Sometimes the water stations were on the right side of the street, sometimes they were on the left side. It did not bother me, because my students were supplying me with ERG. But others I saw. Sometimes they were running on this side of the street and they had to cross to the other side.

And a horrible thing! They allowed the vehicles to travel along the same route. After eleven miles it was so difficult to run. When we had only six miles left, we had to run in the city of Athens. There the traffic was infinitely worse.

You are running this way when, all of a sudden, from the side street cars will enter. Policemen hold the runners and let the cars pass. Here we are dying to reach the destination one minute sooner, and the policeman will say: "Stop!" *7 Oct 1979*

My second morning in Japan I ran about six miles. During the run at least twenty other runners whom I encountered along the way bowed to me in the traditional Japanese manner. Ten or twelve times I also bowed to them. But after that it was too much for me. When they bowed I would just raise my hand to salute them.

Then, when I was really tired, I saw an old lady about sixty years old running. She bowed down, and in her case I felt that I had to bow down also. *1 November 1979*

When I was in Madras, I ran twelve miles in the Madras heat. Afterwards, I went to a store to get some soda. Two, three, four, five, six sodas I drank. The owner laughed and laughed.

I said to him, "Why are you laughing? You go and run twelve miles!"

He said, "I won't be able to run even half a mile."

1 November 1979

After I had run five and a half miles, all of a sudden I saw Jesse Owens' soul around my head, looking at me. It was full of love, softness and tenderness, and I stopped to meditate on the soul.

When I came back from running, one of my students gave me the news that Jesse Owens had died. *31 March 1980*

It is no joke to run a seven-minute pace. Today, in the three-mile race in Greenport, Long Island, by the time the race started at ten o'clock, it was so hot. After the first six hundred metres, I was feeling very hot. My head was so hot, I could not breathe and I was dying of thirst. Still, in my first mile, I did my fastest time since I have been in America: a 6:35 pace. *17 May 1980*

There is an old man who likes me very much. He lives on 150th Street, and he is partially lame. Whenever he sees me running, he has to say something. The other day, about two weeks ago, he stood up from his chair and said, "You are crazy! In this heat you have to run?" *16 August 1980*

In our Oregon race, a man in a wheelchair came first. He defeated the first runner, a top-ranking runner, by sixty metres. I could not believe how fast the man in the wheelchair was going. Then the race organiser told me it always happens like that.

The prizes were so cute. The winners got big pies, which were the same size as their medals. They had a special prize for me, which I wanted to give to the man who was in the wheelchair. When I went near him, he immediately started shedding tears. He was so moved that I was giving the prize to him.

19 October 1980

Yesterday a man saw me running and said, "Dad, Dad, put some life into your running." Then he began showing off, pumping his arms. *25 December 1980*

Two young boys were running. The first time they passed me, they did not see me. Then, when I turned around, one boy told me, "You need some spring, man. You need some spring."

26 December 1980

This morning I was running twelve miles down Main Street to Northern Boulevard. Hundreds of people were waiting for the bus on Main Street; I could hardly run. Then I saw two lame men who were walking with canes, one after the other. I said, "God, I cannot blame You any more. I cannot make complaints to You about my running any more." How could I make complaints to God when I was running so many miles and these two men were walking with canes?

27 March 1981

The day before yesterday I was running back from a four-mile run. A fat old man stopped me and said, "You are still running! You don't want to grow old."

I wish to say that people who aspire will never become old. They will always remain children in the Heart of our Beloved Supreme.

7 April 1981

While I was running in the Boston Marathon, two young men were behind me. Then they passed me and said, "Buddy, come on."

One gentleman said to me, "Friend, my friend, don't give up!"

At one point I was breathing heavily. A little boy came up to me with a few pieces of orange. Usually I do not take oranges, but the little boy was so kind, so I took a piece of orange from him. Then he said, "Don't die, don't die!"

21 April 1981

In Ottawa I went out to run early in the morning. I had been running for about an hour and fifteen minutes when I realised that

I was lost. I asked a very nice and kind-hearted black lady where the Holiday Inn was. She said, "Oh dear, it is so far! Go straight down for at least twenty blocks and then ask people to show you where it is. You won't be able to understand how to get there from here, so after twenty blocks you ask someone where it is."

I ran about twenty blocks to a place that I later found out was only two or three blocks away from the hotel. Unfortunately, when I asked a young boy where the Holiday Inn was, he told me it was in exactly the opposite direction. Instead of telling me it was two blocks in one direction, he turned the other way and said, "Run that way. Go only a couple of blocks—two or three more—and then you will find it." He even pointed the way with his finger.

I ran two or three, then six or seven blocks and still I did not see the hotel. Finally, I approached someone else and said, "Somebody told me that the Holiday Inn was only two blocks in this direction."

The man said, "Not this direction. It is in the other direction. Turn around and go the other way."

I said to myself, "Whom to believe?" The first time, when I was following the young boy's instructions, I was having no doubts. But by this time real doubt had started. O God, what could I do? When one is a stranger, one has to believe in these people. Finally I said, "All right." So I covered six or seven blocks in the other direction, and finally I found the Holiday Inn.   *11 May 1981*

I got a new name today. While I was running, a middle-aged man was driving by in a small van. He was calling out, "Mr. Hill, Mr. Hill!" and looking at me. It seems that everybody has heard of our race on 150th Street, fifty times up and down the hill.

8 July 1981

During a two-mile race in Alley Pond Park, I saw a husband and wife who were also running. After twelve hundred metres the wife was unable to keep pace with the husband, and she wanted to give up. But the husband was encouraging her to continue. He was saying, "This is discipline. If you don't have discipline, you can't accomplish anything."

I thought, "This mantra that he is saying is absolutely descending from Heaven. God is speaking to her through her husband." I was so moved. *21 February 1982*

People who encourage the runners in the Boston Marathon are much more divine than people who encourage runners in many other races. How they cheered us on!

Even before I covered the first mile, I was totally exhausted. You can call it tiredness or hunger or thirst—God knows. After seven miles a little boy stood right in front of me and gave me a glass of water, literally forcing me to drink it.

I said, "How old are you?"

He said, "Four."

So many runners patted me on the back, saying, "Come along, friend, you can make it. Don't give up. Go on, go on, go on!" They were going ahead of me and encouraging me as they passed by. They were very nice people.

The children watching the Boston Marathon were so nice. Little, little children were offering us ice. The people who were spraying us with hoses were my best friends. But some runners did not like it; they got annoyed. Some runners were for water and some were not. I was for water.

An elderly black man and I were running together, and two or three times people got so much joy from drenching us. We two runners were getting new life from the hoses. But other runners were cursing them. They had to go to the other side of the street to avoid the hoses. *19 April 1982*

Today I was buying running shoes. The young man who was selling the shoes was saying that all the shoes were very good, just because he wanted to sell them. When he brought out one particular shoe, he said that he had used this one to run a 4:46 mile. Then he said he had run 800 metres in 1:30. His best time of all was in the quarter-mile, he said. He was bragging that he had done a quarter-mile in 55 seconds—not only once, but twice.

I could not help laughing. I said, "I am an Indian. I did it in 54 and 53.6. Under 54 I did it many times before you were born. I did it without shoes, on a cinder track."

Then he said, "I am so honoured that you have come."

The first time, in 1945, I did the quarter-mile in one minute. Then in 1946 from one minute it came down to 56 seconds, then 55 and then always under 55—54, 53.9 and so on.

28 April 1982

Once in India I was using the starting blocks in a race. When you use the blocks your foot has to touch the ground. You cannot put your foot on the block unless it is also touching the ground. I was 100 per cent sure that my foot was touching the ground, so I was surprised when the official gave me a false start. He said my left foot was not touching the ground.

The official felt sorry for me but he could not tell me what I was supposed to do. He could tell by looking that my left foot was not touching the ground, but he could not say anything to correct it. So I took a standing start, which is useless. Even then I won the 200-metre dash. Then afterwards he saw me on the street and said, "I feel very sorry about your timing."

I said, "I was first."

He said, "That's true, but if you had started from the crouching position, your timing would have been better."

22 August 1982

During the 24-hour race, one runner was telling another runner, "We have to prove that mind can win over matter. But unfortunately, today matter has won." *31 October 1982*

In some ways the Orange Bowl Marathon was worse for me than the Greek marathon. In Greece I did not suffer until after seven or eight miles. Here I began suffering after two miles. Then for six or seven miles it was drizzling, and for the next six or seven miles it was raining heavily. The newspaper said it was raining cats and dogs. Sometimes you could not even see anything in front of you because of the rain. For the first two miles I wore a hat. Then it was so hot that I took it off. "I will manage without it," I said. Then when it started raining so heavily, I did not have the heart to put it back on.

Once while I was walking, an old man who was helping at one of the water stations put a sponge on my head and then brought it down along my spinal column. Such relief! He did not say a word. He just moved the sponge from my head down my spine. He knew how much we were suffering. Everybody looked so pitiful. *24 January 1983*

The morning after the Orange Bowl Marathon, I ran seven miles. That shows what kind of marathon I ran! There was no humidity, and I did not even have to drink. During the marathon sometimes I drank every eight hundred metres!

After five and a half miles I started walking. At that time a man ran by me and said to me, "No walking, no walking!"

Then I started running again, and after half a mile, I saw the same gentleman, walking. I said to him, "It is not good to walk."

He said to me, "But while I was running, I was running faster than you are running!"

So we were two jokers. *24 January 1983*

The other day while I was walking, a gentleman with a cane grabbed my left arm and said, "You are not doing the right thing. You must run, always run!"

I said, "Do you run?"

He said, "I can barely drag my leg, so I can't run."

A nice gentleman! But he did not realise that I also have serious leg problems! *27 April 1985*

The end of the 1000-mile race was on the 6:30 news last night on television. When they mentioned my name they had trouble with "Sri"; they said, "Sir." They called me "Sir Chinmoy, the Queens Fitness Guru." *17 May 1985*

When I used to practise running in the Ashram* when I was young, I used to feel sorry for Mother Earth because my legs were so strong and powerful. I felt I was hurting the ground when I ran. When I did the hop, skip and jump, my hop was so powerful that again I felt I was hurting Mother Earth. But now when I run, I find the ground so hard that it hurts me. Mother Earth should bless me now!

I even feel the difference between the sidewalk and the street. The sidewalk is so much harder than the street. Even when I run on the track at St. John's University, the track hurts my legs.

In the Ashram I used to go out running barefoot at four o'clock in the morning, and I would not even notice that the ground was hard. Then when I went out at six o'clock, after it had become light, I would see pieces of glass in the places where I had been running. So the Supreme had saved me! *10 June 1985*

---

*The Sri Aurobindo Ashram (spiritual community) in south India where Sri Chinmoy lived from the age of 12 to 32.

Often people say they will never run a marathon again. During or after the race they say that this is their last marathon. Then after four days they start thinking about their next marathon. *24 January 1983*

When I run mile after mile, I meditate. When I do not feel like meditating, I sing in silence. I have lists of songs that I play on the double bass, cello, violin, Moroccan instrument, Chinese instrument and harp. There are about forty songs altogether. While running I sing each song inwardly, only once. In this way, when I go out of the house, I do three or four things at once.

This morning at 7:00 I went four miles. I sang very soulfully, in a prayerful way.

When I walk, my mind says, "Once upon a time, you used to walk at an 11 or 13-minute pace. Now you are walking at a 17 or 18-minute pace." So the mind brings discouragement. But then I play a trick on the mind. I say, "Yes, it is a 20-minute pace, but I am gaining in another way. I am meditating longer."

At home I have millions of problems to deal with. In these twenty minutes when I am walking, I am all by myself; so I am very happy. If I take three minutes more, who cares? Nature is helping me. With nature's beauty I am meditating. The mind brings discouragement, but then I tell my mind that for twenty minutes without interruption I am able to meditate. So the mind remains silent. We have to be super-smart when the mind wants to discourage us. *20 May 1984*

If you want to be
A future success,
Then do not allow
Your mind to dwell
On present defeat.

Do not be discouraged.
Give yourself
A second chance.
You will succeed.

Do not be afraid of tasting
The bitterness of failure.
Be brave!
The sweetness of success
Will before long
Befriend you.

Appendix

Biographical Notes on Champion Runners

Jesse Owens, one of the running world's immortal champions, broke three world records and tied a fourth in the span of only 25 minutes at a Big Ten meet in 1935, a feat widely considered one of the greatest athletic achievements of all time. His unprecedented four gold medals at the 1936 Olympics in Berlin undermined Hitler's assertion of German racial superiority. Jesse Owens was a childhood hero to Sri Chinmoy, not only for his physical prowess but for his magnanimity of spirit.

Sudhahota Carl Lewis is one of only four Olympic athletes to win nine gold medals and one of only three to win the same individual event (the long jump) three times. In 1984 he matched Jesse Owens' feat of winning four gold medals, with victories in the 100m, 200m, 4x100m relay and long jump, with additional golds in Seoul in 1988 and Barcelona in 1992. 'King Carl' was named 'Sportsman of the Century' by the International Olympic Committee and 'Olympian of the Century' by *Sports Illustrated*. He received the name 'Sudhahota' when he became a student of Sri Chinmoy in 1983. He very kindly and compassionately encouraged Sri Chinmoy in his own sprinting.

The legendary **Ted Corbitt** was a former Olympian in the 5k, 10k and marathon and often called "the father of long distance running." His "killer weeks" of 200 miles—once over 300 miles in one week—and months of over 1000 miles still inspire younger runners. He continued to compete into his eighties, completing 303 miles in a six-day race at the age of 82. Ted established the official standards for measuring race courses with a calibrated bicycle counter, now used worldwide, and served as chairman of The Athletics Congress National Standards Committee. He was founder and first president of the New York Road Runners Club and president of the Road Runners Club of America.

Dick Beardsley won the Grandma's Marathon in Minnesota in 1980 in 2:09:36 and the London Marathon, a tie, in 2:11. His best marathon time was in 1982 when he duelled with Alberto Salazar in Boston. Ahead of Salazar through the latter stages of the race, Dick traded surges and then sprints during the last mile. Finally, Salazar won with a 2:08:52 to 2:08:53 for Dick, whose time was the fourth fastest ever recorded for the marathon and the fastest non-winning time to that date.

Suprabha Beckjord is one of the most prolific super long-distance runners in the world. She is the only eleven-time finisher in the Sri Chinmoy 3100-Mile Race and is still the only female competitor. Her best is 49 days, 14 hours for 3100 miles, ranking her ninth all-time. In the decade of the nineties, she ran 20,108 multi-day racing miles in fourteen events. She is the American women's record-holder for 700, 1000 and 1300 miles. She was the first woman in the 1996 Sri Chinmoy 2700-Mile Race, establishing new records beyond 1300 miles up to 2700 miles. She won the Sri Chinmoy Seven-Day Race five times, earlier in her career, and has held the women's world record for 1000 miles as well. She has a six-day best of 459 miles, sixth ranking all-time for women.

Eamonn Coghlan, nicknamed the "Chairman of the Boards" for his dominance on the indoor running circuit, held the world indoor best for the mile at 3:49 for many years. He won the prestigious Wannemaker Mile seven times at New York's Millrose Games. He placed fourth in the 1976 Olympics in 1500m and fourth in the 1980 Olympics in 5000m. In 1987 he won the World Championship 5000m race in Rome. A crowd favourite in New York running circles, Eamonn once ran the New York City Marathon to experience a long race with a lot of other people alongside. In 1994 he became the first runner over 40 to break the 4-minute mile.

John Dimick ran 2:11:53 to win the New Orleans Marathon in 1979 and took second place in the 1981 Copenhagen Marathon with a time of 2:15.

Rod Dixon was ranked first in the world in 1979 in 5000m and 2 miles. He received a bronze medal in the 1972 Olympics (1500m) and fourth place in the 1976 Olympics (5000m). He won six major races during 1982, including the Bay to Breakers 7.6-mile race, the Auckland Marathon, the Pepsi 10k Nationals and the Pepsi Challenge 10k. Rod went on to win the New York City Marathon in 1983 in a close duel with Geoff Smith in a time of 2:08:59.

Gary Fanelli was dubbed "the Clown Prince" of road running. He was the first American to win the Umbria, Italy 60-mile, 6-day race (1982) and he won numerous US races as well, including the 1980 Philadelphia 10k, in which second and third places went to Bill Rodgers and Rod Dixon. Also an outstanding half-marathoner (1:03:58) and marathoner (2:14), Gary was more known for his antics of running a marathon dressed up in a suit or other costume. He often ran at the head of a pack of fast runners in a serious competition or set a blistering pace as a rabbit for 10 or 15 miles.

Don Kardong finished fourth in the 1976 Olympic Marathon in 2:11:16 and won the 1978 Honolulu Marathon in 2:17:04. For many years he won or placed high at the Bloomsday Race in Washington State, and later organised it and made the race into a mega-attraction for runners in the Northwest. He was President of the Road Runners Club of America and has written many articles about running and training for magazines and other publications, including *Runners World, Footnotes* and *Running Times.*

Greg Meyer has held the American record for 15k, 10 miles and 20k. His most famous accomplishment was winning the 1983 Boston Marathon in 2:09:00, which at the time was the third fastest in the long history of that race.

Mary Decker Slaney set her first national junior mark in 1974 at 800 metres (2:01.8) as a high school student. Her stellar career lasted over 20 years. She held American outdoor records for 1500m (3:57.12), set in 1983; one mile (4:16.71), set in 1985; 2000m (5:32.7), set in 1984; and 3000m (8:25.83), set in 1985. She set the following American records: 1000m (2:37.6), set in 1989; 1500m (4:00.8), set in 1980; and one mile (4:20.5), set in 1982. She won an exciting World Championships 1500m gold medal in 1983. She was a member of three Olympic teams.

Mike Spino was formerly a track coach at the University of Georgia and at Esalen Institute in California. He is the author of a number of books on running, including *Beyond Jogging* and *The Zen of Running,* and has offered new techniques of concentration, meditation and visualisation to help athletes attain their potential.

Craig Virgin has the distinction of being the only American ever to win the World Cross Country Championship, with back-to-back wins in 1980 and 1981. A fine track and road racer as well, Craig dominated his sport in the USA in the early 1980s. His personal best in the marathon, 2:10:26, gave him a second place finish in the 1981 Boston Marathon.

Cahit Yeter, a prolific racer and marathoner, once ran 2:13 for the marathon in his native Turkey. Later emigrating to the USA, he began a resurgence in his running after an accident had severely damaged his legs. At age 44, he ran 2:26 at the Boston Marathon.

In 1981 he ran 155+ miles in a Sri Chinmoy 24-hour race, setting a North American record. He later set a Masters record for 100 miles on the road (13:33) which stood for several years. He also ran 468 miles in the New York Six-Day Race in 1984.

Robert Zmelik is a Czech athlete who won a gold medal in the Olympic decathlon in 1992 and helped make 'mental conditioning' before a race as popular in the Czech Republic as it had been in the Communist era.

>Do not look backwards
>Or even sideways.
>You will stumble
>And slow your aspiration-pace.
>Run forwards
>With one-pointed concentration
>Towards your Destined Goal.

About Sri Chinmoy

A spiritual teacher from India, Sri Chinmoy came to New York in 1964 and spent more than 40 years creating a unique blend of the traditional wisdom of the East and a dynamic modern Western lifestyle. He conveyed his spiritual insights through an outpouring of books, poems, songs and artwork. Sri Chinmoy was leader of peace meditations at the United Nations and provided guidance in meditation for thousands of students at more than 125 Centres around the world.

Through his own achievements, as well as the founding of the Sri Chinmoy Marathon Team, Sri Chinmoy spent his life vividly demonstrating how sports can be a powerful means to unlock the true potential of the human spirit.

Sri Chinmoy founded the Sri Chinmoy Marathon Team in 1977, and his vision, inspiration, and encouragement were the guiding force behind its growth into what is today the world's largest organiser of endurance events. His innate understanding of the limitless potential that lies within each one of us led him to conceive of endurance events that to others seemed beyond the bounds of human possibility—the prime example being the 3100 Mile Self-Transcendence Race, which has been held annually since 1997 and still remains the longest certified road race in the world.

In his own right, Sri Chinmoy was a formidable athlete, and the dedication which he put into his training inspired his fellow Sri Chinmoy Marathon Team members to expand their own capacities in participating in and organising events. A champion athlete in the spiritual community where he spent his younger days, Sri Chinmoy inspired the Sri Chinmoy Marathon Team through the intensity of his own example, completing a total of 22 marathons and 5 ultramarathons and participating in track-and-field events in Masters Games (including the World Masters Games in Puerto

Rico in 1983 and the World Veterans Games in Miyazaki, Japan in 1993) before injury hampered his running career.

Undaunted, he turned to the field of weightlifting, and soon began setting astounding records which challenged everyone's perceptions as to what was truly possible. His final months on earth saw no halt to his inspirational dedication. Less than two months before his passing on October 11, 2007, Sri Chinmoy succeeded in lifting overhead 800 pounds using only his right arm.

Sri Chinmoy's philosophy is that a balanced lifestyle fosters harmony and inner peace. His integral approach to life encourages physical fitness and sports as a vehicle for personal transformation.

"There are countless people on earth who do not believe in the inner strength or inner life. They feel that the outer life is everything. I do not agree with them," he said. "There is an inner life; there is spirit, and my ability to lift heavy weights proves that it can work in matter as well. I am doing these lifts with the physical body, but the power is coming from an inner source, from my prayer and meditation."

Sri Chinmoy practised sports not only for the joy of it and to keep the body fit, but also because he saw sports as a natural vehicle for expressing his philosophy of self-transcendence. Inspired by his example, several of his students have attempted to stretch their own personal limits by setting new world records in various fields, running multi-day races, swimming the English Channel and climbing some of the world's highest mountains.

For more information about Sri Chinmoy, please visit:
www.srichinmoy.org.

About the Sri Chinmoy Marathon Team

The Sri Chinmoy Marathon Team puts on events for the sporting community in over 20 countries around the world. It is the world's biggest organiser of long-distance ultra running events, and also organises endurance events in other disciplines such as triathlons and lake swims.

The SCMT organises races of all distances from two miles upwards, but it has become most well known for its pioneering work in organising ultrarunning races (races of longer than marathon distance). Many of the races organised by the Sri Chinmoy Marathon Team have now become established favourites in the countries in which they are held. The 24-hour races organised in New Zealand, Switzerland and Great Britain are also the national events for those countries, and the Six and Ten-Day races held in New York every year are extremely popular races in the American ultrarunning calendar. In Australia, the SCMT offers an unparalleled range of multi-discipline events, including the famous Triple-Tri, a triathlon performed three times over in the scenic outskirts of Canberra.

However, the jewel in the Sri Chinmoy Marathon Team's crown is the 3100 Mile Self-Transcendence race, the longest certified road race in the world, which is run each year in New York between June and August.

The SCMT's love of hosting endurance events is a reflection of the core philosophy behind the team's activities. The races are organised on the principles of self-transcendence, where each runner competes against himself and his own previous capacities rather than against his fellow runners. Endurance races allow each competitor to go deep within and truly find the best within themselves in order to persevere and finish, and even though there are trophies for the leading finishers, in truth every runner who completes such long distances is a winner. Over the years, the Sri

Chinmoy Marathon Team has gained a reputation for the level of care and support they provide to the competitors in their races, raising the bar for the level of care in ultra races in general.

For information on how to join a Sri Chinmoy Marathon Team race, please visit:
www.srichinmoyraces.org.

About the World Harmony Run

Sri Chinmoy was the founder and inspiration behind the World Harmony Run, believing that sport is a powerful instrument for promoting global harmony. The World Harmony Run is a global relay that seeks to promote international friendship and understanding. As a symbol of harmony, runners carry a flaming torch, passing it from hand to hand travelling through over 100 nations around the globe. The World Harmony Run does not seek to raise money or highlight any political cause, but simply strives to create goodwill among peoples of all nations.

For more information, please visit:
www.worldharmonyrun.org.

Other Books by Sri Chinmoy

Meditation:
Man-Perfection in God-Satisfaction
Presented with the simplicity and clarity that have become the hallmark of Sri Chinmoy's writings, this book is one of the most comprehensive guides to meditation available. $9.95

Beyond Within:
A Philosophy for the Inner Life
Sri Chinmoy offers profound insight into humanity's relationship with God, and sound advice on how to integrate the highest spiritual aspirations into daily life. $13.95

My Life's Soul-Journey:
Daily Meditations for Ever-Increasing Spiritual Fulfilment
In this volume of daily meditations, each day's offering resonates with the innate goodness of humanity and encourages the reader to bring this goodness to the fore. $13.95

Grace
Sri Chinmoy describes the constant flow of Grace from Above and explains how we can become more receptive to it. $5.00

Compassion
A companion volume on God's Compassion for humanity. $5.00

Forgiveness
Illumining guidance on how to seek divine Forgiveness. $5.00

Love
Sri Chinmoy vividly describes how God loves us more than we can ever imagine. Through his eyes, we begin to fathom the true nature of divine Love. $5.00

The World Beyond
Sri Chinmoy offers spiritual solace and consolation to those who have lost a loved one. $5.00

Death and Reincarnation
In his first extended treatment of the topic, Sri Chinmoy presents his philosophy on death, the afterlife and reincarnation. $7.95

Yoga and the Spiritual Life
Specifically tailored for Western readers, this book offers rare insight into the philosophy of Yoga and Eastern mysticism.

$8.95

The Summits of God-Life:
Samadhi and Siddhi
A genuine account of the world beyond time and space, this is Sri Chinmoy's first-hand account of states of consciousness that only a handful of Masters have ever experienced. $6.95

The Three Branches of India's Life-Tree:
Commentaries on the Vedas, the Upanishads and the Bhagavad Gita
This book is both an excellent introduction for readers who are coming to these Hindu classics for the first time, and a series of illumining meditations for those who already know them well. $13.95

Kundalini: The Mother-Power
Sri Chinmoy explains techniques for awakening the Kundalini and the chakras, warns of the dangers and pitfalls to be avoided, and discusses some of the occult powers that can be developed. $7.95

Everest-Aspiration
Inspired talks on a wide variety of spiritual themes. $9.95

The Inner Promise:
Sri Chinmoy's University Talks
Speaking in a state of deep meditation during these 42 talks, Sri Chinmoy filled the audience with a serenity many had never before experienced. They found his words, as a faculty member later put it, to be "living seeds of spirituality." $14.95

A Child's Heart and a Child's Dream:
Growing Up with Spiritual Wisdom—
A Guide for Parents and Children
Sri Chinmoy offers practical advice on fostering your child's spiritual life, watching him or her grow up with a love of God and a heart of self-giving. $7.95

The Master and the Disciple
Sri Chinmoy says in this definitive book on the Guru-disciple relationship: "The most important thing a Guru does for his spiritual children is to make them aware of something vast and infinite within themselves, which is nothing other than God Himself."

$7.95

Siddhartha Becomes the Buddha
The combination of profound insight and simplicity of language makes this book an excellent choice for anyone, young or old, seeking to understand one of the world's most influential spiritual figures. $6.95

Music by Sri Chinmoy

Flute Music for Meditation

While in a state of deep meditation, Sri Chinmoy plays his haunting melodies on the echo flute. Ideal for inspiration in your personal meditation. CD, $12.95

To Order Books and Music by Sri Chinmoy

Sri Chinmoy's books and music are available worldwide, with his writings often available both in English and in translation in many countries. To order books within the U.S., please contact:

Heart-Light Distributors
(800) 739-2885

or visit:
www.srichinmoybooks.com
which has contact information for on-line booksellers and for distributors in countries outside of the U.S.